A BRAVE AND VIOLENT THEATRE

MONOLOGUES, SCENES AND CRITICAL CONTEXT FROM 20TH CENTURY IRISH DRAMA

Edited by
Michael Bigelow Dixon & Michele Volansky

FOREWORD BY
BERNARD FARRELL

A Smith and Kraus Book

Published by Smith and Kraus, Inc.
One Main Street, Lyme, NH 03768

Copyright © 1995 by Smith and Kraus, Inc.
All rights reserved
Manufactured in the United States of America
Cover and Text Design by Julia Hill
Cover Photo by Amelia Stein © 1994

First Edition: May 1995
10 9 8 7 6 5 4 3 2 1

Library of Congress Cataloging-in-Publication

A Brave and Violent Theatre : monologues, scenes, and critical context for 20th century Irish drama /
edited by Michael Bigelow Dixon & Michele Volansky.
     p. cm.
     Includes bibliographical references.
     ISBN 1-880399-71-7

     1. Monologues. 2. Dialogues. 3. Acting. 4. Irish drama -- 20th century. I. Dixon,
Michael Bigelow. II. Volansky, Michele.

PN2080.B73   1995
822'.041089415   94-42036
                               CIP

ACKNOWLEDGEMENTS

*The editors would like to thank the following list
of contributors from Actors Theatre of Louisville
whose research made this volume possible:*

Deidre Clemente
Liz Engelman
Kristi Halvorson
Dottie LaBry
Tanya Palmer
Christopher Shinn
Valerie Smith
Matthew Southworth
Michelle Spencer
John Stinson
Jim Valone
Anita Vassdal
Isabelle Vinaches

ACTORS THEATRE OF LOUISVILLE

Founded in 1964, Actors Theatre of Louisville has evolved under the artistic leadership of Producing Director Jon Jory since 1969. In its three-theatre complex, ATL presents its annual Humana Festival of New American Plays, Classics in Context Festival, Flying Solo & Friends Festival of cutting-edge solo and ensemble performance, and the biennial Bingham Signature Shakespeare series. ATL annually mounts more than 30 productions and is the recipient of the most prestigious awards bestowed on a regional theatre: a special Tony Award for Distinguished Achievement, the James N. Vaughan Memorial Award for Exceptional Achievement and Contribution to the Development of Professional Theatre, and the Margo Jones Award for the Encouagement of New Plays. ATL has been named the State Theatre of Kentucky and has performed in more than 29 cities in 15 countries.

EDITORS' NOTE

Once again, a treasury of drama and criticism has emerged from a monologue project at Actors Theatre of Louisville. Last time the subject was Restoration Comedy of Manners. This time it's Irish theatre of the 20th century. And what a hundred years it's been for Irish playwrights! Beginning with those who envisioned a literary renaissance — Yeats, Synge, and Lady Gregory — and ending with a great number of accomplished authors — Friel, Leonard, Farrell, and Murphy, to name a few — this century of Irish drama has excelled in those very qualities that make for exciting theatre — a fiery spirit, feisty humor, political daring, imaginative myth, formal experimentation, and vernacular lyricism.

As forms, the monologue and two-character scene (excerpted from longer plays) have proven ideal in tapping the broad spectrum of ideas and expression that characterize this prolific century of theatre. To examine a nation's drama thoroughly, of course, is the work of a lifetime, and for most of us not possible. Fortunately, it's also not essential; for to appreciate 20th century Irish drama, one can sample the work — and that's where a book such as this becomes useful. This volume can be combed for audition and scene-work material, or referenced for leads on single plays to be produced. Yet for those who are neither actor nor producer, this volume can be enjoyed as an introduction to Irish thought and talent, to concerns and character, to a subversive humor and rebellious spirit that made survival possible through centuries of occupation and intermittent famine.

No matter what its use, however, one word of advice must be offered regarding the lyricism of Irish plays: These works were written to be spoken — on stage, alone, or in company (don't be shy!), for the song of Irish drama is best sung aloud.

— Michael Bigelow Dixon and Michele Volansky

CONTENTS

ACKNOWLEDGMENTS v

EDITORS' NOTE vii

FOREWORD: LOVING ACTING
  by Bernard Farrell 1

CRITICAL CONTEXT

The History and Geography of Modern Irish Drama
  by Stephen Watt 6

Writing Plays in Ireland Today
  by David Nowlan 22

MONOLOGUES

TWENTY-FOUR MONOLOGUES FOR WOMEN

  Happy Days by Samuel Beckett 37

  Richard's Cork Leg by Brendan Behan 38

  The Holy Ground by Dermot Bolger (2) 39

  Low in the Dark by Marina Carr 43

  Coggerers by Paul Vincent Carroll 44

  After Easter by Anne Devlin 45

  The Queen's Enemies by Lord Dunsany 46

  The First Mrs. Fraser by St. John Ervine 47

  Canaries by Bernard Farrell 48

  Lovers by Brian Friel (2) 50

  Donny Boy by Robin Glendinning 53

  Spreading the News by Lady Gregory 55

  Says I, Says He by Ron Hutchinson 56

  Step-in-the-Hollow by Donagh MacDonagh 57

  Maeve by Edward Martyn 58

  The Guernica Hotel by Jim Nolan 60

  The Plough and the Stars by Sean O'Casey 62

  The Shadow of a Gunman by Sean O'Casey 64

  Belfry by Billy Roche (2) 66

  In the Shadow of the Glen by John Millington Synge 69

  The Tinker's Wedding by John Millington Synge 70

TWENTY-SEVEN MONOLOGUES FOR MEN

   Endgame by Samuel Beckett 70

   Richard's Cork Leg by Brendan Behan (2) 72

   Design for a Headstone by Seamus Byrne 75

   The Glittering Gate by Lord Dunsany 76

   John Ferguson by St. John Ervine 77

   Lovers by Brian Friel 79

   Philadelphia, Here I Come! by Brian Friel 80

   Translations by Brian Friel 81

   Grania by Lady Gregory 82

   Hanrahan's Oath by Lady Gregory 84

   Eejits by Ron Hutchinson (2) 85

   The Moon in the Yellow River by Denis Johnston 92

   The Old Lady Says "No!" by Denis Johnston 93

   The Scythe and the Sunset by Denis Johnston 94

   The Field by John B. Keane 95

   The Death and Resurrection of Mr. Roche by Thomas Kilroy . . 97

   The Bending of the Bough by George Moore 99

   The Guernica Hotel by Jim Nolan (2) 101

   Moonshine by Jim Nolan 104

   Belfry by Billy Roche (2) 106

   What is an Irishman? by George Bernard Shaw 110

   The Shadowy Waters by William Butler Yeats 112

   The Unicorn from the Stars by William Butler Yeats 114

SCENES

NINE SCENES FOR ONE WOMAN AND ONE MAN

   After Easter by Anne Devlin 117

   Lovers by Brian Friel 121

   Translations by Brian Friel 124

   Exiles by James Joyce 128

   The Patrick Pearse Motel by Hugh Leonard 132

   Youth's the Season by Mary Manning 135

   Moonshine by Jim Nolan 139

   Playboy of the Western World by John Millington Synge . . . 144

   Deirdre by William Butler Yeats 148

FIVE SCENES FOR TWO WOMEN

    Richard's Cork Leg by Brendan Behan 153

    After Easter by Anne Devlin 157

    Sive by John B. Keane. 162

    Youth's the Season by Mary Manning 166

    Bailegangaire by Tom Murphy 168

FOUR SCENES FOR TWO MEN

    Waiting for Godot by Samuel Beckett 175

    Forty-Four Sycamore by Bernard Farrell. 181

    The Shadow of a Gunman by Sean O'Casey. 185

    John Bull's Other Island by George Bernard Shaw 188

PERMISSION ACKNOWLEDGMENTS 193

LOVING ACTING
by Bernard Farrell

In the seventies, I was part of Dublin's Lantern Theatre Workshop trying desperately — like many others — to discover if I had a place in the theatre. I knew I wanted to be a playwright and yet, whenever an actor was late for rehearsal, I'd be first on the stage to read-in.

Clearly there was an actor within me — and it took me a long time to discover that "within me" was exactly where he should stay.

The realisation came during my greatest Read-In performance — in a new play that offered a whole range of conflicting (and unexplained) emotions — and, at a dramatic moment, I had passionately flung the script aside to attack these emotions when the director cried out: "Bernard, for God's sake just read it and stop trying to act."

"Trying" was the word that finished me — and returned me to playwriting and, I am happy to say, that within a year I had written my first play for the Abbey Theatre. But something good came from my humiliation: a respect and, indeed, a love of actors.

Fourteen plays later this affection has not faded — although at times it has been sorely tested!

Some of the plays I write are quite vicious — although comic — and at one particular audition, I kindly took an actor aside to give him advice. He had been called-back several times and I whispered that perhaps what the director was missing was the aggression in his performance. "Ah," he said, "he wants to see that, does he? Excellent."

Minutes later, he roared into the room, kicked over a chair, stalked us like a caged animal, snarled his lines — while grinding his car keys deep into the paint-work on the walls. I looked on in horror and, beside me, the director whispered, "What the hell did you say to him?"

In the end, he got the part and was wonderful. But more recently his name came up for a new play and he was being short-listed until someone said, "But can we afford to paint the rehearsal room again?"

Almost as exciting as the room-wrecking actor is the I-can-do-that actor. No task or stage business is ever given a moment's thought. "Walk on stilts? — I can dance on stilts." "Ride a one-wheeled bicycle? — I can ride a no-wheeled bicycle." "Fall from the flies onto my spine and then tap-dance? — Done it a million times."

In fairness, I only experienced one extreme case of this — and not on the stage but in a BBC television series I wrote.

The actor was asked, "You do drive, don't you?" She stood back, offended, "Of course I drive." And then she turned to me and whispered, "Where can I learn to drive before Thursday?"

When Thursday came, the only people who knew about her crash-course (!) were myself and my cowriter. So when the director told her to drive the car fast towards the camera (and crew) and then come to a screeching stop and she said "Fine," I knew that my career and their lives were about to end.

She was asked to do it three times. Each time she came inches closer to killing them — and when the director called "Wrap" and patted her head, she walked to me, all smiles, and said, "You don't have aspirin, do you?"

An inverted form of the same behaviour occurred in the Abbey when, having rehearsed for five weeks in a "house" with a marked-in staircase, we moved on the set with the real stairs. That wonderful actor, May Cluskey, now sadly gone from us, looked at the stairs and said, "I'm not expected to climb that, am I?" Someone said "Yes" and May levelled him with a look: "With *my* arthritis?"

For May, I rewrote the scene.

Even if none of these aspects of the actor's life endeared them to me, I would still be won over by the Hamlet who bestrides the stage for two hours and then stands in the bar, drink in hand, with the ice tremulously tinkling in his glass, as he tries to engage in tortuous conversation. Or the on-stage Blanche who, off-stage, will blanch at the merest hint of comment and disappear terrified into the night.

And who would not love those who submit themselves to auditions — delivering pieces (perhaps from this collection) and awaiting the cold, echoing "Thank you" or, Yes!, the glorious "Can you stay back please?"

Perhaps, for me, the love is also born of something that is rooted in the memory of an afternoon in the Lantern Theatre Workshop when I thought that I, too, could be an actor...and was told to stop trying.

The difference, of course, is that actors, real actors — the ones who can chill our blood or raise our hackles or who can simply reduce us to wide-eyed children — would never have stopped trying.

And that, above all, is what makes them wonderful.

BERNARD FARRELL IS AN IRISH WRITER OF PLAYS FOR THE THEATRE, television and radio, who lives in County Wicklow, south of Dublin. His playwriting career began in 1979 with the debut of his first work, *I Do Not Like Thee, Doctor Fell* at the Abbey Theatre. His plays have been produced in Dublin on both stages of the Abbey Theatre, The Gate, the Gaiety Theatre, the Lyceum and TEAM UC Theatre. His plays have also been produced throughout Ireland and several have premiered at the Red Kettle Theatre Company in Waterford. Subsequent to their Irish premieres, his works have been produced in the USA, Canada, UK, Belgium, Holland, Germany and Australia. These works include: *Legs Eleven* (1979), *Canaries* (1980), *All In Favour Said No!* (1981), *Petty Sessions* (1983), *Don Juan* (from Molière, 1984), *Then Moses Met Marconi* (1984), *All The Way Back* (1985), *One-Two-Three O'Leary* (1985), *Because Just Because* (1986), *Say Cheese!* (1987), *Forty-Four Sycamore* (1992), *The Last Apache Reunion* (1993), and *Happy Birthday Dear Alice* (1994).

Bernard Farrell has been Writer-in-Residence with TEAM UC Theatre Company and is a recipient of The Rooney Prize for Irish Literature. His radio and television plays have been produced by both RTE and the BBC.

CRITICAL CONTEXT

THE HISTORY AND GEOGRAPHY OF MODERN IRISH DRAMA

by Stephen Watt

"The Irish are accused of never forgetting, but
that is because the English never remember."

— *Declan Kiberd*

Following in the two thousand-year shadow of the Roman philos-pher Horace, who in his *Ars Poetica* asked if a poem is born *ab ovo* or "made" by the society in which it is produced, I want to sketch a few ways in which Ireland has "made" or fashioned its playwrights. In other words, what has being Irish meant to a distinguished tradition of twentieth-century writers from William Butler Yeats and James Joyce earlier in the century to such contemporary novelists and poets as Bernard Mac Laverty Jennifer Johnston, Seamus Heaney, and Eavan Boland — and, more specifically, to such prolific dramatists as Tom Murphy, Brian Friel, John B. Keane, and Frank McGuinness? Although numerous answers recommend themselves, two in particular seem both obvious and significant: One concerns collective or national memory; the other, the compass points of a geography of longstand-ing import to Irish literature. And while delineating how these histori-cal and geographical factors have helped shape modern Irish culture, I shall try to focus on the twentieth-century Irish theatre in the years preceding the rise of contemporary drama described by David Nowlan in this volume. For while his great enthusiasm for the Irish theatre after about 1960 is amply justified by the achievements he cites, not long before the period he refers to as marking "the greatest renaissance of Irish drama in history" was one in which little, if any, Irish play-wrighting of note existed. How a modern Irish drama was born — and a "renaissance" of contemporary playwriting was subsequently influ-enced by this birth — is the real subject of this essay.

My narrative begins not with History, but with several kinds of particular histories, because if such dramatists as Friel and McGuinness share anything both with each other and with the Irish writers who have preceded them, it is their abiding concern with European history, theatre history, and, most acutely, the history of a troubled relationship between England and Ireland, colonizer and colonized. In response to this predictable observation — the near obsession of Irish writers with the past — Declan Kiberd, cultural critic at University College Dublin from whom I have taken my epigraph, perhaps has put it best: "The Irish are accused of never forgetting, but that is because the English never remember."[1] Precisely *how* one remembers the past — or, as the present disputation in intellectual circles would have it, how one *revises* it — is a matter beyond the scope of this essay.[2] I want merely to underscore the inflection of Ireland's literary production by its colonial history, a phenomenon really without parallel in contemporary American or British drama. (With the exceptions of such topics as Vietnam or the AIDS crisis on the American stage, how many plays of, say, Harold Pinter or Sam Shepard, Marsha Norman or David Mamet, involve national history?) In Friel's canon, such dramas as *The Freedom of the City* (1973), which depicts the aftermath of a 1970 peace march very much like those that occurred in Derry City at the time, and *Translations* (1980), a play about the Anglicizing "translation" of rural locales into a more readable colonialist geography, "remember" both recent and more remote pasts marked by the British presence in Ireland. More subtly, *Dancing at Lughnasa* (1990) recalls rural Donegal in the 1930s and a past constituted of both Celtic and Christian traditions on the verge of being displaced not by imperial rule, but by an encroaching industrialism which will forever alter local economies and destroy families like the Mundy's.

To take another example, McGuinness's *Observe The Sons of Ulster Marching Toward the Somme* (1985) represents the historical relationship between Northern Irish Protestants and Britain, portraying the enormous "blood sacrifice" made by Ulster loyalists in World War One at the Somme. Such a commitment of lives, a kind of counter to the rising of a predominantly Catholic insurrection of nationalists on Easter, 1916, served the purpose of furthering a security which Ulster Protestants regarded as "resting on a contract with the British crown."[3] This colonial history — and sectarian tension — seems never too far away in Irish drama, even in plays like McGuinness's *Someone Who'll Watch Over Me* (1992) which, on the surface at least, has very little to do with the centuries of a British presence in Ireland. One such instance in McGuinness's play is the pointed, partially absurd exchange over the Great Famine of the nineteenth century between Edward and Michael, the Irish Catholic and British prisoners held by terrorists in present-day Lebanon in which the action is set:

Edward: Remember the Famine? The Great Hunger?

Michael: The Irish Famine was a dreadful event. I don't
dispute its seriousness. But I'm sorry. How can
I be personally responsible for what happened
then? It was a hundred and fifty fucking years ago.

Edward: It was yesterday.

Michael: You are, ridiculous, Edward.

Edward: I am Irish.[4]

And being Irish, as Sean O'Casey's character Jack Boyle reminds his drinking buddy Joxer in *Juno and the Paycock* (1924), in part means that "We don't forget, we don't forget them things. . . . If they've taken everything else from us, Joxer, they've left us our memory."[5]

What things do Irish writers remember in their literature? While few historical events can rival the magnitude of the Great Famine in the Irish collective memory — a historical tragedy that has led to, among other works, Liam O'Flaherty's novel *Famine* (1937), Patrick Kavanagh's magnificent poem "The Great Hunger" (1942), and Tom Murphy's play *Famine* (1968) — many have become concretized in the Irish consciousness into veritable monuments that parallel the stature of certain well-known dates and places for many Americans. Just the mention of 1776 or 1865, of Wall Street in 1929, Pearl Harbor on December 7, 1941, or Dallas in 1963 triggers a flood of associations. So it is with the Irish: The defeat of Catholic troops by William of Orange at the Boyne River in 1691, which marks the origin of the term "Orangemen" or Northern Protestant loyalists; the rising of the United Irishmen in 1798 to seize control from the British; the Fenian strikes against England in the 1860s and the Home Rule Movement later in the century; the rising on Easter Monday, 1916, and subsequent execution of nationalists who organized it; the civil war in the 1920s over the independence of Ireland and the partitioning of the island; and — more recently — the "Bloody Sunday" in Derry on January 30, 1972, when thirteen civil rights marchers were killed by British paratroopers. These and similar events have occupied Irish writers throughout this century.

It is hardly an accident that at roughly the same time the Home Rule Movement of the 1880s stalled with the downfall of Charles Stewart Parnell in 1891, a downfall replayed with great emotion over Christmas dinner in Joyce's *A Portrait of the Artist as a Young Man* (1916), Irish writers and intellectuals were contributing to an incipient cultural renaissance. That is to say, although Parnell's decline seriously damaged prospects for realizing Ireland's *political nationalism*, a lively *cultural nationalism* was only in its infancy. This movement involved a rekindling of interest in the Irish language and a republication for a modern audience of Celtic mythology. In the late 1870s, Standish O'Grady published his *Bardic History of Ireland*, and throughout the 1890s Irish scholars and artists returned to native literature and the Irish language for inspiration. The Irish National Literary Society was formed in 1892; Douglas Hyde lectured on "The Necessity for de-Anglicizing Ireland" and spearheaded the founding of the Gaelic League in 1893; and Arthur Griffith began his nationalist newspaper *The United Irishman* in 1899, among other significant cultural events. And, most important for our purposes, the conversations between William Butler Yeats, Lady Gregory and Edward Martyn in 1897 led to the Irish Literary Theatre's first season in 1899 and, in 1904, to the Abbey Theatre. From its earliest productions, the Irish Literary Theatre, whose leadership later included John Millington Synge, was strongly committed to a cultural, if not a more strenuous, nationalism.[6] Such an ideological commitment was destined to reverse the provincial status of Ireland which, theatrically speaking, until the rise of the Abbey was little more than a satellite of the London stage.

Such was the case at the close of the nineteenth century, when the young James Joyce (born in 1882) and Sean O'Casey (born in 1880) became interested in drama and theatre. During the 1890s, the Theatre Royal, Gaiety Theatre, and Queen's Royal Theatre, Dublin's three professional venues at the turn of the century (along with several variety houses), produced only a handful of original Irish plays.

Instead, particularly at the Theatre Royal and the Gaiety, Dublin served as one- or two-week stops for stars from the London stage, for Italian and German opera companies, and, usually at the Queen's Theatre, for popular native touring companies mounting a repertory of crowd favorites.[7] Joyce, for instance, saw the great Mrs. Patrick Campbell as Hermann Sudermann's notorious "fallen woman" Magda and as Paula Tanqueray in Sir Arthur Wing Pinero's *The Second Mrs. Tanqueray* (1893); and was apparently quite taken with Olga Nethersole, later prosecuted in New York for her suggestive performances as a seductress in the American playwright Clyde Fitch's *Sapho*, adapted from the Alphonse Daudet novel.[8] Given this state of affairs, it is scarcely surprising that in Joyce's monumental novel *Ulysses* (1922), set in Dublin in 1904, Leopold and Molly Bloom's recollections of going to the theatre are of seeing British actors in mostly British plays: Martin Harvey, Herbert Beerbohm Tree, Mrs. Millicent Bandmann-Palmer, and others. Celebrated actors such as Harvey, Frank Benson, and Henry Irving toured Dublin regularly during this period, typically mixing their favorite Shakespeare roles with more contemporary ones designed to exhibit their stage qualities to best effect. These attractions, along with opera and the annual Christmas pantomimes, dominated bills at both the Theatre Royal and the Gaiety Theatre.

Meanwhile, the adolescent and working-class O'Casey, later to provoke rioting at the Abbey Theatre with his critique of the Easter rising, *The Plough and the Stars* (1926), was viewing more rough-and-tumble versions of Shakespeare and the melodramas of one of the nineteenth century's most popular artists, Dion Boucicault. Boucicault, a native Irishman who moved to London and then America, was revered in Dublin for such plays as *The Colleen Bawn* (1860), *Arrah-na-Pogue* (1865), and *The Shaughraun* (1874), performed nearly every year at the Queen's Royal Theatre (and, occasionally, at the other Dublin houses) throughout the 1890s and the inaugural decades of this century. As his career evolved, Boucicault became increasingly preoccupied with Irish nationalism and with overturning derogatory stereotypes of Irishmen on the stage, especially that comical, blarney-talking, and whiskey-drinking figure known as the "Stage Irishman" (a figure who surfaced from time to time in American films of the 1930s and 40s as played by Victor McLaglen and one-time actor at the Abbey Theatre, Barry Fitzgerald).[9] Boucicault's nationalist fervor was shared by such other melodramatists between 1890 and the 1920s as J. W. Whitbread, Hubert O'Grady, Ira Allen, and P.J. Bourke, many of whose plays commemorate the lives of nationalist leaders of the past — Wolfe Tone, Edward Fitzgerald, and Henry Joy McCracken of the 1798 United Irishmen, for example — or represent famous events in Ireland's history.[10] Such exciting dramas typically offered a mostly working-class audience sensational scenes of lavish stage effects, brave heroes and their despicable adversaries (informers being the worst of this lot), comic business, musical interludes, and a solid evening's entertainment for their money. But the Queen's Royal Theatre, conveying patriotic melodrama to a loyal, if untutored, segment of the playgoing public, lacked the support of a more refined audience, and finally could not spark the kind of cultural renewal for which the Abbey Theatre became famous.

Cultural nationalism at the Abbey Theatre, however, often grew into something more, and the theatre became known for both its staunch nationalism and, later, with the plays of Synge and O'Casey, for its occasionally volatile "ructions" when writers like O'Casey questioned or debunked nationalist ideals. The politics of Yeats's *Cathleen ni Houlihan* (1902), an allegorical drama set in 1798 which ends with a young man abandoning his family to help a symbolic Mother Ireland rid her "house" of strangers, seems clear and straightforward; as old Mother Ireland is successful in recruiting her sons to come to her aid, she is transformed into a youthful and beautiful queen. This ideology of the sanctity of dying for one's country permeates the rhetoric of Padraic Pearse, one of the leaders of Easter 1916 uprising. His poem "The Mother" summarizes this sentiment:

I do not grudge them lord: Lord, I do not grudge
My two strong sons that I have seen go out
To break their strength and die, they and a few,
In bloody protest for a glorious thing,
. . . .
    And yet I have my joy:
My sons were faithful and they fought.[11]

Ten years after the failed 1916 rising, with sections of Dublin levelled by the shellings of British gunboats and the lives of many of his countrymen lost, O'Casey interrogated Pearse's nationalist fervor in

The Plough and the Stars, the production of which on the third night of its run was interrupted by the riotings of an audience that took "violent exception" to what D.E.S Maxwell terms O'Casey's "political nihilism."[12] His earlier successes at the Abbey, *The Shadow of a Gunman* (1923) and *Juno and the Paycock*, certainly presented militant nationalism with ironic and undercutting humor, yet for a variety of reasons, both achieved considerable success. Not so with *The Plough and the Stars*, which sharply questioned the sacrifice paid by men and women during the Easter rising. O'Casey suggested his rejection of Pearse's politics in Act Two of the play by juxtaposing the mythology of a heroic martyrdom to the tawdry negotiations in a pub between a clownish man and a desperate prostitute. Public debates (and censure) followed, and the play was closed with O'Casey eventually leaving the Abbey and moving to England.

This turbulent time in Irish history is revisited frequently in contemporary Irish literature. Bernard Mac Laverty's novel *Cal* (1983), adapted in 1984 by Pat O'Connor for a film of the same title, includes a scene in which the young Cal McCrystal, caught up in IRA violence and reluctant to participate any further, is confronted by Skeffington, a superior who attempts to bring him back into the fold. Skeffington recites the very lines from "The Mother" I have quoted above, to which Cal immediately responds, "But it is not like 1916."[13] And, as I have suggested earlier, in MacGuinness's *Observe the Sons of Ulster*, written some sixty years after O'Casey's incendiary drama, the Northern Protestant version of Pearse's discourse on heroism is announced by Pyper, an Ulsterman fighting for the British in World War One and a survivor of the Battle of the Somme, who opens the play with the proclamation, "The sons of Ulster will rise and lay their enemy low, as they did at the Boyne, as they did at the Somme, against any invader who will trespass on to their Homeland. . . . Sinn Fein? [This means] Ourselves alone. It is we, the Protestant people, who have always stood alone. We have stood alone and triumphed, for we are God's chosen."[14] Here McGuinness builds his play from well-known historical materials, just as Friel more recently turns to the life of Gaelic Ireland's greatest leader Hugh O'Neill in *Making History* (1988). Like O'Casey, I would argue, Friel and McGuinness are forged in the crucible of Anglo-Irish history. And whether their plays concern Middle Eastern terrorists, bag ladies and factory workers, or the residents of rural Ballybeg, this sense of history pervades their writing and much fine Irish writing today.

I'll return to Irish playwrights' deep knowledge of another kind of history — that of the modern European theatre — in a moment, but before doing so I want to move to my second point about the geography of Irish literature. From the above discussion and from, for example, Friel and McGuinness's emotional and literal proximity to the border that separates Northern Ireland from the republic, one might expect my point about geography to be plotted along a North-South axis. (Friel was born in County Tyrone, grew up in Derry, and spent many happy summer days in the small village home of his mother's family in rural Donegal, which becomes the imaginary Ballybeg of what are arguably his greatest plays, and still maintains his residence there. McGuinness was born in Donegal and lives in Dublin, where most of his plays have had their premieres.) To say that both writers have been affected by the "Troubles" in the North would be to belabor the obvious; and in addition to his writing, Friel, who has served in the Irish Senate, has attempted to analyze the impact of this history on his countrymen. In 1980, this project led to his cofounding with actor Stephen Rea of The Field Day Theatre Company, dedicated through its productions, publications, and other educational activities to providing a "fresh analysis" of the complex "interweave" of "political and cultural (largely literary) forces. . .stimulated by the pressure of the existing poltical crisis" in the North.[15] Field Day has collected, for example, a massive three-volume edition of the history of Irish writing and in 1991, as part of the activities memorializing the 75th anniversary of the 1916 Easter Rising, published *Revising the Rising*, a collection of scholarly essays that attempts to reposition this event within the context of contemporary Ireland.

But while all of this reinforces the importance of North and South to Irish politics, it perforce remains silent on the equally significant cultural valences of its counterpart, the East-West axis. In *Fictions of the Irish Literary Renaissance* (1987), John Wilson Foster refers to "an ancient and lingering expression of an east-west cleft in the Irish cultural psyche," and such a divide, it seems to me, is especially evident not only in Friel's plays (although not necessarily for the more general reasons Foster adumbrates), but also in Irish literature from the very beginning of this century.[16] In dozens of plays at the Abbey, portrayals of life in small, usually western, villages advance a cultural opposition between city and country, between present urbanization and past serenity, between the corrosive influence of the colonizer and the vestiges of a traditional culture largely untouched by British incursions, modern technologies, and — as is the case in Friel's *Translations* — the English language itself. Among others Lady Gregory, a resident of Galway, and Synge, a chronicler of life in County Mayo and on the Aran Islands just off the Galway coast, wrote a number of so-called "peasant plays" for the Abbey: Plays like Synge's *The Well of the Saints* (1905) and *The Playboy of the Western World* (1907), and Gregory's *Twenty-Five* (1903) and *Spreading the News* (1904) which celebrate a simple, albeit difficult, life vastly different from the bustle of life in Dublin. Most of Synge's plays, as David Krause argues in his fine study *The Profane Book of Irish Comedy* (1982), pit desire or the pleasure-principal against the cold repressions of Catholicism as represented by the "Saint" in *The Well of the Saints* and the laughable Shawn Keogh in *Playboy*, who, out of fear of temptation and Father Reilly's condemnation, refuses even to stay in the same shebeen with Pegeen Mike until they are married in the Church.

Among the features of Abbey Theatre peasant drama, therefore, are an opposition between an archaic, lively, pre-Christian culture and the inevitable repressions brought about by religion;[17] a simple, yet eloquent language in which English and Gaelic expression are mixed in unique syntaxes and figurative constructions; and a closer, unalienated relationship with and appreciation for the natural beauty of the Irish countryside. Compared to the working-class residents of O'Casey's urban tenements — or the paralysis of Joyce's more refined, if also more neurotic, bourgeois Dubliners — Synge's and Lady Gregory's peasants represented all that remained of a simpler time and more pristine place many associated with native Irishness. Such a life, of course, as evidenced by Synge's *Riders to the Sea* (1904), could also contain tragedy, as Aran Islanders travelling to fairs in Galway and other sites on the west coast of Ireland to sell or barter their goods braved treacherous waters to conduct their business. This short play of Synge's — with its evocation of an almost ritualistic pattern of death, its aversions to folk superstitions and primitive domestic economy, and its poignant conclusion with the sounds of women keening for another young man lost to the sea — marks a major achievement of the Abbey's inaugural season and of Synge's all-too-brief life. In sum, the Ireland in which *Riders to the Sea* and many of Synge's and Lady Gregory's plays are set is an authentic, green world on the opposite side of the country from Dublin. It is into this world that Gabriel Conroy, the Europeanized protagonist of Joyce's story "The Dead" from *Dubliners* (1914), must travel if he is to discover the homeland that, until his epiphany at the end of the story, he has never before cared to know.

And, of course, in contemporary Irish literature, especially that written amid the turbulence of the North like Mac Laverty's *Cal* and Jennifer Johnston's *The Railway Station Man* (1984), the west serves as a pastoral respite from the nightmare that is recent history in Northern Ireland. From her artist's cottage in Donegal, Helen, the widowed protagonist of Johnston's novel whose husband was killed on the streets of Derry, perhaps puts it best in her comparison of the two locales:

> I remember occasionally . . . the shuddering of the houses when the explosion happened. Windows, then, taken by surprise, cracked, some even splintered to the ground and for days the smell of smoke lingered in unexpected places.

But now, here, the glass holds.[18]

And moments later, recalling the night her husband died:

> In the distance the fire-engines raced to a fire, ambulances, army vehicles. Glass cracked and split. The flames burst out through windows flickering into the streets.

[Now] I was startled by my own happiness. The first thing I did after I bought this cottage was to build a small glass porch onto the front, not so much to protect me from the wind, but so that I could walk past packed shelves of plants each time I used the front door. . . .

I sold everything that had been in the house in Derry. . . . (p. 11)

The East-West cleft, as Foster calls it, thus acquires a vastly different resonance — performs very different cultural work — in Ireland after the "Troubles" of 1968, but is nonetheless still a crucial component in representations of contemporary Irish life.

Friel knows this and is careful not to romanticize green, rural Ireland any more than nationalists have romanticized the glories of dying for the cause of an independent Ireland. He even parodies overestimation of primitive Ireland in his satirical drama *The Communication Cord* (1982), when two young men conspire to impress the father of one of their girlfriends by drawing upon the charms of an "authentic reproduction" of a peasant cottage. Referring to the cottage, one friend tells the other, "This is where we all come from. This is our first cathedral. This shaped our souls. This determined our first pieties."[19] This simulation can only exercise the intended effect and deception in the larger context of at least a century of such depictions of the west. And I might add that one of my favorite plays from the contemporary Irish theatre (and one of David Nowlan's as well, as he acknowledges) — John B. Keane's *The Field* first produced in 1966 — is similarly cast against an East-West opposition that resides deep within the Irish cultural psyche. Absent this representational context — and the history of privations suffered by tenant farmers during the Famine, when thousands of peasants in the west were thrown off of the fields they cultivated — Keane's protagonist Bull MacCabe would hardly seem so tragic; his play, hardly so magnificent.

Just as many of Lady Gregory's thirty-seven plays between 1907 and 1927 and most of Synge's originate in the Irish peasantry of the West — both, like Yeats and George Moore, also turned to Celtic mythology in their work — so too what is perhaps Friel's greatest play, *Dancing at Lughnasa*, emanates from this cultural or intellectual geography.[20] In the process of making a few very brief comments on Friel's play, I would like also to return to an earlier point about another history shared by Friel and many major figures in that great contemporary "renaissance" of Irish play writing: Namely, their long experience and study of modern dramatic form, particularly that of Henrik Ibsen and Anton Chekhov. Both Friel and McGuinness have adapted Chekhov's *Three Sisters* for the Anglo-Irish stage (Friel in 1982 and McGuinness in 1990), and McGuinness has written versions of Ibsen's *Rosmersholm* (1987) and *Peer Gynt* (1988). There is, in one sense, nothing unusual about this: Both Bernard Shaw and Joyce wrote about Ibsen — Joyce's first publication as an eighteen-year-old college student was on Ibsen's *When We Dead Awaken* — and, more recently, Thomas Kilroy has adapted both Ibsen and Chekhov for the Irish stage.[21] But the presence of Chekhov, it seems to me, is everywhere in *Dancing at Lughnasa*: The feeling of *The Cherry Orchard*, for example, with its melancholic sorrow for an era passing slowly out of existence as symbolized by the haunting sounds of a violin string snapping discordantly and an ax wreaking its destruction in the distance. As in Chekhov's play, there is no holding back so-called "progress" and an uncertain, foreboding future. Indeed, like Chekhov, Friel creates a strong sense of several characters' profound ill-suitedness for the ascendant social order and the changes it promises. How *could* Agnes and Rose Mundy ever have survived in London? As we learn, only with great difficulty. How could Father Jack survive in the new Ballbeg for long? He does not. How could the family remain intact? It cannot. Yet, as refracted through Michael's memory and softened by time, all that remain by the end of the play are the dance and a "dream music that is both heard and imagined" (p. 71). Or so it seems in Michael's memory, as the threnody for a happy way of life on the wane gives way to a warmer feeling that "owes nothing to fact" (p. 71).

Unlike Chekhov, Friel makes all of this clear through another specifically modern framing device built into the structure of *Lughnasa*, that of the memory play with its novel-like narrator looking back on a time gone by. Michael Mundy in Friel's play provokes comparison with Tom Wingfield in Tennessee Williams's *The Glass Menagerie* and, less obviously, with such narrators as Henry Carr in Tom Stoppard's *Travesties*. My point here is that in a play like *Dancing at Lughnasa*, one written by such a consummate student of dramatic form as Friel, Irish concerns — poverty, celibacy in rural areas like Ballybeg due to widespread immigration, advancing industrialization which effectively ends the cottage industry of glovemaking in the Mundy household — meet the sophisticated sensibilities of a master theatrical craftsman. The result is one of the most beautiful plays of the contemporary theatre.

This appropriation and adaptation of dramatic forms to convey an Irish subject are familiar artistic procedures in the history of modern

Irish drama. For his poetic renditions of episodes in Celtic mythology, plays like *On Baile's Stand* (1904), *At the Hawk's Well* (1916) and the later *The Death of Cuchulain* (1939), Yeats combined the innovative decorative ideas of Gordon Craig's "New Stagecraft" with musical effects from Japanese Nō drama and various techniques from the French Symbolists. After the second and third decades of this century brought with them an explosion of realistic drama, *The Plough and the Stars* for instance, O'Casey moved to expressionist drama in such plays as *The Silver Tassie* (1928), influenced by German writers like Ernst Toller. And in 1930 the European avant-garde found a new home in Dublin in Hilton Edwards' and Micheál MacLiammóir's Gate Theatre, a theatre opened with the expressed purpose of producing experimental and noncommercial drama.[22] Though plagued with financial problems within a few years of its opening, the Gate also encouraged such important Irish dramatists as Denis Johnston and Austin Clarke, thus supplementing, though never surpassing, the Abbey in its development of modern Irish dramatists.

The making of the modern Irish playwright, therefore, involves the dynamic interplay of Ireland's past with its present, the communication of persistent Irish concerns by varied dramatic forms developed in over a century of modern theatre, and an uncanny ear for the music of English as it is spoken in Ireland. It involves the negotiation of a tradition and a history that can never be forgotten with a geography that seemingly must always be traversed between the brilliant emerald landscape and the modern city. Needless to say, I have failed to mention more writers than I have been able to discuss here; but with the possible exception of the mystical Theosophists at the beginning of the century, perhaps best represented by the writings of George Russell (AE) and Yeats in his more spiritual moments, the vast majority of Irish writers with whom I am familiar, at some time or another, inevitably confront both the history and geography that have defined Irish culture. And one result of this confrontation has been the writing of some of the most important plays of the modern theatre.

STEPHEN WATT IS AN ASSOCIATE PROFESSOR OF ENGLISH AT Indiana University. His publications include: *American Drama: Colonial to Contemporary* (1995), cowritten with Gary A. Richardson; *Joyce, O'Casey, and the Irish Popular Theater* (1991); *When They Weren't Doing Shakespeare* (1989), edited with Judith L. Fisher. His works in progress include: *Marketing Modernisms,* edited with Kevin J. H. Dettmar, forthcoming in 1996; *Arthur Kopit: A Casebook* (1997), a book-length study of postmodern theatre; and a study of theatrical representations of Ireland in the nineteenth century.

NOTES

1. Declan Kiberd, "Anglo-Irish Attitudes," in *Ireland's Field Day*. (London: Hutchinson, 1985), p. 93. For a fuller discussion of this issue, see Ulrich Schneider, "Staging History in Contemporary Anglo-Irish Drama: Brian Friel and Frank McGuinness," in *The Crows Behind the Plough: History and Violence in Anglo-Irish Poetry and Drama*, ed. Geert Lernout (Amsterdam/Atlanta: Rodopi, 1991), pp. 79-98.

2. One influential volume of revisionist Irish history is *Revising the Rising*, eds. Máirín Ní Dhonnchadha and Theo Dorgan (Derry: Field Day, 1991). This collection of eight essays is dedicated to rethinking the Easter, 1916 nationalist uprising in Ireland on the occasion of its seventy-fifth anniversary.

3. Edna Longley, "The Rising, The Somme and Irish Memory," in *Revising the Rising*, p. 37.

4. Frank McGuinness, *Someone Who'll Watch Over Me* (London: Faber and Faber, 1992), p. 30. All further quotations from this play will be taken from this edition and cited parenthetically in the text.

5. Sean O'Casey, *Collected Plays*, 4 vols. (New York: St. Martin's, 1949), 1: 25. A five-volume *The Complete Plays of Sean O'Casey* was published by Macmillan in 1984.

6. Among the numerous theatre histories available on the topic of Irish theatre at the turn of the century, see D. E. S. Maxwell, *A Critical History of the Modern Irish Drama, 1891-1980* (Cambridge: Cambridge University Press, 1984), esp. pp. 1-59; and Hugh Hunt, *The Abbey: Ireland's National Theatre, 1904-1979* (Dublin: Gill and Macmillan, 1979).

7. For a discussion of the Dublin stage before the rise of the Abbey, see my *Joyce, O'Casey, and the Irish Popular Theater* (Syracuse: Syracuse University Press, 1991), pp. 1-88. For specific titles and productions, see the "Dublin Theatrical Calendar 1898-1904," pp. 201-239 of the same volume.

8. Much of this information can be found in Stanislaus Joyce's account *My Brother's Keeper: James Joyce's Early Years*, ed. Richard Ellmann (New York: Viking, 1958). For a study of Olga Nethersole's career and the scandal over *Sapho*, see Joy Harriman Reilly, "A Forgotten 'Fallen Woman': Olga Nethersole's *Sapho*," in *When They Weren't Doing Shakespeare: Essays on Nineteenth-Century British and American Theatre*, eds. Judith L. Fisher and Stephen Watt (Athens: University of Georgia Press, 1989), pp. 106-20.

9. For a thorough discussion of stereotyping of the Irish on the British stage, see Richard Allen Cave, "Staging the Irishman," in J. S. Bratton, et al, *Acts of Supremacy: The British Empire and the Stage, 1790-1930* (Manchester: University of Manchester Press, 1991), pp. 62-128.

10. For a critical discussion of these plays and the reprinting of four exemplary scripts, see Cheryl Herr, ed. *For the Land They Loved: Irish Political Melodramas, 1890-1925* (Syracuse: Syracuse University Press, 1991).

11. Padraic H. Pearse, *The Collected Works of Padraic H. Pearse* (Dublin/London: Maunsel, 1918), p. 64.

12. Maxwell, p. 102.

13. Bernard Mac Laverty, *Cal* (New York: George Braziller, 1983), p. 73.

14. Frank McGuinness, *Observe the Sons of Ulster Marching Towards the Somme* (London: Faber and Faber, 1986), p. 10.

15. Seamus Deane, "Introduction" to *Nationalism, Colonialism, and Literature* by Terry Eagleton, Fredric Jameson, and Edward Said (Minneapolis: University of Minnesota Press, 1990), p. 11.

16. John Wilson Foster, *Fictions of the Irish Literary Revival: A Changeling Art* (Syracuse: Syracuse University Press, 1987), p. 8.

17. David Krause discusses this opposition in his *The Profane Book of Irish Comdy* (Ithaca: Cornell University Press, 1982), esp. pp. 17-170.

18. Jennifer Johnston, *The Railway Station Man* (London: Penguin, 1984), p. 2. All further quotations from Johnston's novel come from this edition and will be cited parenthetically in the text.

19. Brian Friel, *The Communication Cord* (London: Faber and Faber, 1983), p. 15.

20. All quotations from Brian Friel's *Dancing at Lughnasa* come from the Faber edition (London, 1991) and will be followed by page numbers in the text.

21. For a discussion of Kilroy's work, including these adaptations, see Christopher Murray, "Worlds Elsewhere: The Plays of Thomas Kilroy," *Éire-Ireland* 29 (Summer 1994): 123-38.

22. For a brief discussion of the Gate theatre, see Maxwell, pp. 131-33.

Writing Plays
in Ireland Today
by David Nowlan

It seemed simple enough when I was young and becoming addicted to theatre in the forties and fifties: Ireland had a great literary and dramatic heritage and we who were lucky enough to have inherited the tradition could look to such as Sean O'Casey and John Millington Synge as the icons of contemporary urban and rural drama respectively. William Butler Yeats could be respected as the creator of a distinctive poetic drama and if it was better poetry than it was theatre, so be it. It was still distinctively literary and we Irish had a great way with words, did we not? And, we could boast, the tradition ran back much further into history.

In the immediate past, as it were, we could glow in the glory of Oscar Wilde and George Bernard Shaw while, much earlier, we could lay claim to the dramatic mastery of the likes of George Farquhar, Richard Brinsley Sheridan and Oliver Goldsmith. We did not, in those days, think much of Dion Boucicault, although we came to admire his melodramatic talent and theatrical skill a couple of decades later. But we did not, at the time, think much about new Irish playwrights, or even admire much the journeymen dramatists of that and the immediately preceding decades when Brinsley McNamara, Lennox Robinson and, later, Louis Dalton, Denis Johnston, M. J. Molloy, John McCann, Paul Vincent Carroll and more were turning out a great variety of plays varying from the comedy pot-boiler through the deeply felt melodrama to the adventurous avant-garde.

As an audience, we seemed happy to rest on our playwrights' historic laurels. We were remarkably unaware that we were on the threshold of what was to become the period of the greatest renaissance of Irish drama in history. If there were ten or a dozen new Irish plays in any year of the fifties we reckoned productivity (if not always quality) was high, and we were still glad to revel in reproductions of Wilde,

O'Casey, Goldsmith, Synge and the rest of the inherited galaxy. We hardly noticed the advent of a striking new peasant dramatist called John B. Keane, a bar-owner in the town of Listowel, Co. Kerry, whose *Sive* and *Sharon's Grave* — two almost operatic melodramas about the tradition and the terror of rural Irish life — came to the stage via the amateur drama movement. Yet Keane was to go on to write one of the best Irish plays of this century (*The Field*, which is a much finer, leaner play than is apparent from its overblown movie version) and to be recognised belatedly for the quality and integrity of his earlier works.

Paradoxically, we were to recognise the new renaissance primarily by way of the success of two new Irish plays in such places so culturally distant as London and New York. Brian Friel had written several good plays before his *Philadelphia, Here I Come!* became a smash hit in the old Helen Hayes Theatre on Broadway, and Hugh Leonard had done some very good work before his *Da* had a similar New York success. In a way, those two dramas — the first about exile (a theme that was to recur in many of Friel's subsequent plays) and the second about the family (again, a recurring theme in Leonard's later work) — were perceived at home as manifestations of the inheritance of the rural legacy of Synge and the urban legacy of O'Casey, now enjoying international acclaim just as the plays of Synge and O'Casey had done before them.

Irish audiences still tended to look overseas for validation of the quality which they thought they saw in new Irish writing for the stage, and media reaction at home tended to underlie this domestic insecurity. The play that was exported successfully simply had to be great and the play which may well have been enjoyed at home found it difficult to gain such esteem if it did not go on to international fame or fortune. And, of course, the Irish plays which succeeded abroad tended to be those written in the literary tradition of the past even when they were dealing with wholly contemporary Irish themes. Foreign audiences tended to recognise the quality of Irish drama when, even in the sixties and seventies, it echoed the shape and substance and literary rhythms which had their origins in the 19th and early 20th centuries of Irish stage writings. Our playwrights still had a great way with words as far as the standard-setting foreigners were concerned.

But that was to change quite soon. Brian Friel, it was, who was first heard to argue that Irish dramatists should be writing primarily for Irish audiences. "We should be talking to ourselves," he said at the time he was involved in the founding of the Field Day production company. Ironically, the play which he wrote for its inauguration was *Translations* — very much a domestic work about the linguistic colonisation of Ireland by the English — went on to huge success in Britain and lesser but not insignificant notice in the United States. But the notion that an Irish playwright did not have to write for Broadway or West End audiences took root and, therewith, the stage was philosophically set for the recognition at home of the explosion of dramatic writing that had already started in Ireland.

I have written already that a year in the fifties which saw the arrival of a dozen or so new Irish plays was reckoned a good year. Last year there were more than 50 new Irish works on offer in Irish theatres, between 10 and 20 of which were notable local successes. That seems to this reviewer to be a remarkable output from a population of five million people. And what is more remarkable about this current profusion of new Irish drama is that much of it does not carry echoes of the famous Irish literary tradition. Neither, it should be said, does a great deal of it fit in easily to the earlier themes or issues with which Irish writers were generally expected to deal.

Just as Ireland has moved, politically and socially, from a close and conservative peasant society to full membership of the greater European community in a remarkably small number of decades, so Irish theatre has moved to a more cosmopolitan perspective. In terms of construction and presentation, the visual presentation of ideas is now as acceptable as their literary manifestation (at least partly as a result of the importation into the Dublin Theatre Festival in recent decades of highly visual modes of production from such places as Poland and France and the USA). Yet words and their rhythms also are still deeply appreciated by Irish audiences and marvelously offered by Irish actors and directors. Nowhere in the world, I would submit, are the plays of Samuel Beckett (another of the icons of the Irish literary dramatic tradition who himself moved to the image as well as the word) received with such rhythmic verbal resonances as they are in a native production in Dublin.

So what is there to say of the current plethora of Irish playwrights? First and foremost, it is necessary to record the huge sense of privilege which this reviewer feels about being so lucky to be alive and going to the theatre when so much is going on. Secondly, I don't believe it is possible to identify any particular trends, dramatically or socially, in the contemporary works which find their way on to Irish stages, or to stages further afield. What we are enjoying is a great variety of distinctive Irish voices expressing themselves theatrically in a great variety of different theatrical ways. By no means are all of them being heard or seen beyond the boundaries of Ireland, yet they have greatly widened Irish theatrical horizons.

Simply to list them all would take up more space than can be provided in this book. In time, some serious academic work may analyse the impulses and trends which have led fifty or more current Irish playwrights to create the words and images which now enrich the Irish theatres. Then we may learn about how Sebastian Barry, for instance, has inherited some of the poetic theatrical sensibilities of both the genuinely rural M. J. Molloy and the adoptively rural J. M. Synge, yet is still very much his own person offering an individual lyrical vision of both theatre and society. We might discover how Martin Lynch came from a deeply political involvement in republican Belfast to use theatre to explain to people in his parish what their position in life really was. Or how the more overtly theatrical Marie Jones came to pen and produce her much more vaudevillian vision of the same geographical and political situation with particular reference to the women in her society.

J. Graham Reid (who, alas, has since moved from live theatre to television to express his deeply felt and sharply perceptive ideas of the recent turmoil of Northern Ireland) has been another contemporary voice — this time drafted from the ranks of school-teaching — from the north of this small island in such works as the deeply touching *Remembrance* and the sharply frightening *Death of Humpty Dumpty*. Christina Reid, among the small legion of Northern dramatists, seems more than most to have set out from a consciously theatrical starting point, yet it is hard to identify her individual dramatic heritage. And few of us who had the opportunity of experiencing it at first hand will forget the delicate whimsy of the late Stewart Parker in his exploration of contemporary northern Irish conflict and its roots in political history — a wholly contemporary voice prematurely silenced by death. His advent to theatre was heralded by a deep interest in pop music. How does one try to place that within the traditions of Irish drama?

Moving south across the political (but emphatically not the cultural) border we come first, in a merely geographical line, to the farmer, Eugene McCabe, from the border county of Monaghan, whose *King of the Castle* excited Dublin audiences in the early sixties with its exposition of a woman trapped in a rapacious middle-class farmer's possessiveness and in the temptation of a young labourer. He moved on later to more obviously literary endeavours, including an exploration of the life of Jonathan Swift, and then (alas again!) to television before going back to the farm. Maybe Ibsen was his dramatic progenitor (as he was James Joyce's in that author's only foray into drama) but what place has that theory in the heritage of Irish drama?

There is little trace of Ibsen in most of the rest of contemporary Irish playwrights. But there may be traces of Chekhov in some of them — a dramatic heritage which is conceivably traceable to the common or parallel origins of the establishment of the Abbey Theatre in Dublin and the Arts Theatre in Moscow. Brian Friel, without question the master of contemporary Irish writing for the theatre, has not only adapted Chekhov's own work to an Irish mode (and has also adapted Turgenev for the stage) but has written several original works whose theatrical forebears could plausibly be argued to be Chekhovian. *Aristocrats*, his tale of a family of the Irish "big house" falling on leaner times, is probably the most obvious example, but there are similar echoes in other works of his. Yet the finest of his writing for the stage, best manifest in the miraculous *Faith Healer*, surely has no discernible origins in either Irish or Russian drama. It is Friel's own structure (four consecutive yet overlapping and conflicting monologues) and his own agonising about the burdens of artistic creativity.

Probably Brian Friel's most globally successful play has been *Dancing at Lughnasa* — another examination of decline and exile, infused with a liveliness and loveliness, which has proved universally enlivening — and the director who first directed that work for the Abbey Theatre in Dublin (and in London, New York, Sydney and elsewhere) was Patrick Mason, currently artistic director of the Abbey Theatre. Mason was also seminally involved in some of the work which led the nonliterary, primarily visual or mimic emergence of (to Ireland) new forms of dramatic expression. The author most identified with this sea-change in Irish drama, many of whose plays were directed by Mason, is Tom McIntyre, whose plays have ranged from the wholly nonverbal *Jack Be Nimble* to the quintessential and elegantly literary *Kitty O'Shea*. Between those two there have been excursions into mixtures of mime and dance and verbiage exploring both mythical and historical Irish stories, adapting both poetry (Patrick Kavanagh's epic poem *The Great Hunger* comes most to mind) and mythology to primarily visual theatrical form.

It may have been this development within the perceived "establishment" of Irish theatre which opened the way for other authors to craft works that owed nothing to Irish literary traditions yet were deeply concerned with current Irish social and cultural issues. Author-director Gerald Stembridge springs forcefully to mind in this context as one of the archetypal disciples of a credo which says that Irish theatre should be addressed to Irish audiences. It is doubtful that Stembridge's work will ever be seen on stages outside of Ireland unless the man moves to other communities to pursue his personal vocation of providing hilarious and contemporaneous theatrical expositions of social concerns in whatever community he happens to be working. But his productions of, for instance, Shakespeare's *Macbeth* for clowns or of *The Comedy of Errors* as an Irish country-and-western entertainment (staged, significantly, on the hallowed traditional ground of the Abbey Theatre) offers some measure of the extent to which mainstream Irish theatre has moved from its perceived literary traditions. And this movement has been used by many younger dramatists in Ireland to explore on stage some of the social and historical issues which concern (or should concern) the people who live on this island.

Hugh Leonard has probably been the master craftsman of Irish drama since the fifties and was the first high-profile playwright to hone in on the hitherto fallow ground of suburbia. His richest and most emotionally rewarding works have usually been drawn from autobiographical sources, as in *Da* and *A Life* or *Summer*. But his interests have ranged more widely than those of many other Irish dramatists (he has written an excellent farce about Sherlock Holmes called *The Mask of Moriarty*, for instance) and his modes of theatrical expression have varied more than most, ranging from the traditional "realism" of Irish writing in the earlier part of this century to pastiches of French farce and on to intricate time plays like *Moving*, in which a slight re-arrangement of history between acts one and two alters the shape and purpose of a very ordinary suburban family.

Bernard Farrell, one of the more prolific and entertaining of the contemporary native dramatists, appears more than most others to be following the lineage of Leonard, yet has carved his own niche in his use of dark comedies to explore the frailties of the Irish middle classes. From the group encounter session of his first play, *I Do Not Like Thee Dr. Fell*, through the anarchic farce about trade unionism, *All In Favour Said No*, to the deep seriousness of a reunion of old school buddies in *The Last Apache Reunion*, which explored the nastiness of bullies, and his latest, *Happy Birthday Dear Alice*, in which an old woman triumphs over her uncaring family. These comedies have all done a great deal to tell Irish audiences about the kind of society in which they are living.

Then there was the emergence within the past two decades of The Passion Machine, a very socially conscious production company established by a group of school teachers, led by Paul Mercier and Roddy Doyle, to give voice to the constituents of the north city, working-class area in which they taught. Very funny plays about young unemployed drifters (*Wasters* or *Brownbread*, in which three young kids kidnap a bishop because they reckoned they had nothing much better to do), about the local football team, *Studs*, who never win any matches, staged in balletic slow motion for most of the time, or *War* — a piece about the extraordinary social phenomenon of quiz competitions in bars. These and many more, mostly written by Mercier and Doyle themselves, have played to packed and delighted audiences in Dublin, and I can identify no precedent in the traditional Irish drama canon.

Other newly established production companies have also nurtured new voices speaking in differing accents. The Druid Theatre in Galway drew heavily on what might loosely, but inaccurately, be described as the Synge tradition and, indeed, offered a brutal and cruel interpretation of *The Playboy of the Western World*, which has almost become the definitive version of the classic. But they were also exploring new forms and have continued to do so, even as they offered Jacobean drama and Italian contemporary farce and more. Currently, they are touring with the latest work by Vincent Woods, a new playwright who casts his plays in deeply rural myths and customs with many of the most striking dramatic effects vested in such very old street-performance traditions as mummers and "straw boys."

Probably the playwright most enduringly associated with the Druid (although most of his work has actually been presented by the Abbey) is Thomas Murphy who remains, outside of Ireland, the least recognized of Ireland's major dramatists. He has written a vast body of work, much of it deeply metaphysical, almost poetic and constantly challenging to both intellect and emotion. His first major success was with the physically frightening and grittily realistic *Whistle in the Dark*. That was to be followed by the darkly whimsical surrealism of *The Morning After Optimism,* in which we find a prostitute and her pimp wandering in a forest. Murphy's own professed favourite is a historical epic on the horrific potato famine called, simply, *Famine*. But for me his greatest triumphs have been later works: *The Gigli Concert*, in which an unhappy property developer consults a quack therapist so that he may be enabled to sing like Benjamino Gigli, is a magnificent monument to finding the human spirit triumphant in the most unlikely circumstances; and *Bailegangaire* (staged by the Druid with the late Siobhan McKenna giving the last, and one of the greatest, performances of her distinguished career) which was a symphony for three female voices — a senile mother bedded in the family kitchen and her two deeply unhappy adult daughters.

Murphy's is a highly individualistic voice in Irish drama, breaking molds in both content and construction. Frank McGuinness, on the other hand, seems much more orthodox as he goes his cosmopolitan way from success to success. Yet his very cosmopolitanism is itself unusual in the mainstream of Irish drama. He started out with a very simple well-made play called *The Factory Girls* about women in a shirt factory going on strike. Then came his strikingly original exploration of the roots of protestant attitudes in Northern Ireland in *Observe the*

Sons of Ulster Marching Towards the Somme, and then an exposition of *Caravaggio* quite unlike anything he had done before, and a version of *Peer Gynt* and a quietly eccentric comedy of an odd south Dublin family in *The Bird Sanctuary* and his internationally successful *Someone Who'll Watch Over Me* based on the experiences of the people held hostage in Beirut. It is impossible to predict where next his typewriter will settle.

Billy Roche seems a great deal more predictable, yet no less successful. The first four of his plays were actually first staged in London by the Bush Theatre and the Royal Shakespeare Company, yet each one of them has Roche's home town of Wexford embedded under every character's fingernails, so place-specific are they. Very much in the mold of the old-fashioned "well-made play", they explore small-town relationships in such specific detail that they become universally recognisable: *A Handful of Stars* was about the young kids hanging around the local equivalent of the pool hall and getting into trouble with the local constabulary, while *Poor Beast in the Rain* was set in the local bookie's shop and dealt with relationships in post-adolescence and *Belfry* was set in the local church where one of the married parishioners is tempted into a relationship with the sacristan. Roche's latest work — *The Cavalcaders* — is centered on the closing of a local shoemaker's shop and the friendships of a group of men who enjoy singing in close harmony. Since the author himself was a member of a musical group in his hometown, authenticity is, as in the other plays, the order of the night.

And still more playwrights keep appearing on the Irish scene. Declan Hughes writes eclectically and effectively for Rough Magic, another of the more innovative production companies, but is as likely to focus on Dashiell Hammett and Lillian Hellman as on an Irishwoman who has problems in her relationship with her dead mother. Jimmy Murphy emerged from the ranks of house-painters (as Brendan Behan had done before him) to craft *Brothers of the Brush*, one of the most dramatically accomplished first plays that I have seen in five decades of theatre-going, about trade unionism among a group of painters working for a crooked boss in the black economy during times of high unemployment. As has often been the case in Irish drama, comedy is the vehicle upon which the more serious ideas are carried. And in the just completed Dublin Theatre Festival there emerged that relative rarity in Irish theatre — a strikingly original female voice (Marina Carr) with a perspective on the world and on Ireland that differs sharply from those of the male playwrights who have so dominated the scene up to now. Her play, *The Mai*, is about four generations of women in one family and how they relate to the world around them.

The catalogue could go on and on, and still there would be no apparent shape to it. It should include Thomas Kilroy who has been writing original dramas since the fifties, as well as being a professor of English in Galway University, and has provided us with such as *Talbot's Box*, a stylist study of the seemingly masochistic Matt Talbot who went about with chains around his body and who has since been beatified by the Catholic Church, or *Double Cross*, which looked at the contrasting and conflicting figures of William Joyce Lord Haw Haw of the Nazi radio propaganda machine in the second World War, and Brendan Bracken who was one of Churchill's prime polemicists during the same conflict. Both Joyce and Bracken were, of course, Irishmen. And the same Kilroy has also wrought an admirable translocation of Chekhov's *The Seagull* to an Irish great house setting.

So, where is the pattern in that? Or in Frank McGuinness's output? Or in the greatly varied output of all the writers mentioned, and many more besides? Maybe there is no pattern at all. What has happened is simply that, as Ireland has moved rapidly from a relatively closed society to a much more modern community, Irish theatre has exploded in as many social and dramatic directions as can be imagined. Some of the plays are very distinctively Irish and recognisable within the frame of the older theatrical traditions of Irish play writing. Others could have originated in any one of several countries or cultures, and many could be adapted relatively easily from an Irish to another setting. If there is a clearer pattern than that, I am unable to define it. In any case, there is far too much going on to be wasting time analysing it. Much better to be out and about and enjoying a richness of theatre that was neither evident nor present when I was cutting my theatrical teeth as a devoted audience. That devotion has paid off handsomely now and I am grateful to the dozens and dozens of authors, actors, directors, and designers who have made it possible.

DAVID NOWLAN IS DRAMA CRITIC OF *THE IRISH TIMES,* DUBLIN.

TWENTY-FOUR MONOLOGUES
FOR WOMEN

HAPPY DAYS
by Samuel Beckett

Winnie, a woman about fifty, is buried in a pile of sand up to her neck. Here, she reaches out to her silent husband Willie in a desperate attempt to receive reassurance and affection.

WINNIE:

(Murmur.) God. *(Pause. WILLIE laughs quietly. After a moment she joins in. They laugh quietly together. WILLIE stops. She laughs on a moment alone. WILLIE joins in. They laugh together. She stops. WILLIE laughs on a moment alone. He stops. Pause. Normal voice.)* Ah well what a joy in any case to hear you laugh again, Willie, I was convinced I never would, you never would. *(Pause.)* I suppose some people night think us a trifle irreverent, but I doubt it. *(Pause.)* How can one better magnify the Almighty than by sniggering with him at his little jokes, particularly the poorer ones? *(Pause.)* I think you would back me up there, Willie. *(Pause.)* Or were we perhaps diverted by two quite different things? *(Pause.)* Oh well, what does it matter, that is what I always say, so long as one...you know...what is that wonderful line...laughing wild...something something laughing wild amid severest woe. *(Pause.)* And now? *(Long pause.)* Was I lovable once, Willie? *(Pause.)* Was I ever lovable? *(Pause.)* Do not misunderstand my question, I am not asking you if you loved me, we know all about that, I am asking you if you found me lovable — at one stage. *(Pause.)* No? *(Pause.)* You can't? *(Pause.)* Well I admit it is a teaser. And you have done more than your bit already, for the time being, just lie back now and relax, I shall not trouble you again unless I am compelled to, just to know you are there within hearing and conceivably on the semi-alert is...er...paradise enow.

RICHARD'S CORK LEG
by Brendan Behan

The Bawds, Irish prostitutes, are in a cemetery in Dublin where beggars and prostitutes gather to conduct their business. They are entertaining themselves as they wait for prospective clients to come along.

BAWD II:

I was in a convent one time and our donkey dropped dead outside the laundry. He must have been thinking about the other thing because his person was very prominent so to speak. So the gardener said he'd cut it off so as the children wouldn't be looking at it hanging off the dead donkey like a man's arm over the side of a boat. So he cut it off and threw it over a wall, where did it land only in the nun's garden. So there it was and the holy nuns came out to walk round and say their prayers. And this nun sees it and she lets a scream out of her and calls another nun, "Oh, Sister Dolores, come here and look at this." So Sister Dolores comes and she calls another nun. "O Sister Theresa of the Little Flower come here at once and look at this," and Sister Theresa of the Little Flower lets a scream out of her and calls another nun, "Oh, Sister Most Holy Passion come here at once and look at this," and they were all standing looking at the donkey's destructor when the Reverend Mother comes out. "My children," she says, "what is the trouble?" So they point to the ass's tool lying on the path and the Reverend Mother bursts into tears and cries "Oh, look what the Protestants did to poor Father Slattery."

THE HOLY GROUND
by Dermot Bolger

*Monica is a woman in her late fifties, living in a suburb of present day
Dublin. Her unhappy, childless marriage ends with her poisoning her
husband Myles, a man who grew increasingly cruel and distant over
the years. She has just returned from his funeral and is sorting
through his possessions.*

MONICA:

Who would have thought back then? The day we walked all the way
out to the Poolbeg lighthouse with you not speaking. Me thinking, this
is it, we're going to break up. My heart was down in my boots because...you made me feel special Myles, not just a heifer at a mart. You
turned to me — I'll never forget that stare — like you were about to
commit murder. Then I knew suddenly. You were helpless. You did-
n't know what to say. "Myles," I said. You closed your hand over mine.
And when you took it away I felt the shape of the box. I didn't know
what to say...so I said "Yes." Just like that. Looked at you there, like
you were about to blubber and I loved you, Myles. You were my child,
under that big frame, and I swore I'd look after you and keep you from
harm. He had everything planned. He was good that way — desposits,
installments. I didn't know the half of it. There was no need for me to.
This house within a roar of Tolka Park, this same furniture...all calcu-
lated, down to the shilling. The table and chairs already bought. The
beds from his mother's farmhouse. The cradle that had been his.
   Our wedding night he was so gentle. Only other person I ever
slept with was Deirdre, sharing that little flat when we first came to
Dublin. I missed her now and the girls in work; fingering his socks,
wanted to ask someone how often to wash his pyjamas. The little
names we had for each other, the way we'd make excuses to go to the
bathroom. Sometimes we were so polite we'd start giggling at the
table. So little I knew about men really, so little if anything he knew
about women. He came in from a match and looked at my face.
Myles' s voice: "Oh, my God, are you in pain, is it a miscarriage?"
Woman's voice: "Myles," I said, "it's my friend has come."
Myles' s voice: "Deirdre?"
Woman's voice: My time of the month Myles. Women bleed, it's
   painful, do you understand?" I could see his face clouded.

Myles's voice: "Did I do wrong? Does that mean...?"

Woman's voice: "It takes time," I said. "Time."

Myles's voice: "When can we try again?"

Woman's voice: Those few days Myles, you were someone else. Then, when it was time, you were rougher, I wasn't ready. It was...more like a challenge. It hurt. *(Pause.)* And every time it hurt more.

THE HOLY GROUND
by Dermot Bolger

In a living room in Drumcondra, an old suburb of North Dublin, a woman in her fifties has finished packing up her husband's papers and photographs. She's exhausted as much from the activities of this funeral day as she is by her revelation in this monologue.

MONICA:

I woke on Tuesday and knew something was wrong. The little sword of light under my door almost paled with dawn. And every step I took seemd a descent into nightmare. I stood outside this door, Myles, and realized...I wasn't afraid you were dead, I was afraid you might still be alive. You were slumped here in front of the perpetual lamp *(She looks down at the carpet.)* a grotesque, pitiable figure. All the years in the GPO, Myles, the second hatch on the right after the statue of Cuchulainn. It wasn't Rosie Henderson I saw now, but that statue of a warrior dying, tying himself to a rock. For half an hour I stood in this doorway like the men of Ireland, afraid to approach, not daring to call your name in case you'd look up. Then...I went walking through the streets in my slippers and dressing gown. *(She crosses stage to stand behind his armchair.)*

Outside the Mater Hospital two nurses appeared. They brought me inside and phoned an ambulance. "Was it the rat poison?" I kept asking, "the rat poison?" I wanted to be charged, to be taken away. *(She pauses, trying to remember the word.)* What was it the doctor called it? "Warfarin." I think that was the name. *(A strong male voice.)* "Your husband died from a clot to the brain. The man had a history of thrombosis, he'd take treatment from nobody. Rat poison contains warfarin that prevents clotting and thins out the blood. If you did give it to him you probably lengthened his life. Go home now Mrs. O'Muirthile and keep your mouth shut." *(She sits down in his armchair for the first time.)* Sweet Jesus, Myles, what sort of wife was I? I couldn't make you happy in life and I couldn't even send you to your death. They thought it was for you I was crying but it was for me. Because how can I cope thrust into the world, how can I learn to watch that *(She glances at the television.)* without hunching up beside it, to walk out into the evening like an ordinary person? To learn to play bingo and sit in the park, to chance a conversation with a kind person on the bus? *(She seems to sink further and further into the armchair.)*

The doctor sent in an old nun in white robes to comfort me. She pressed her hands into mine. "Pray," she said. Those kind eyes she had, she made me feel warm. "Our Father who art in heaven," she began. I closed my eyes and thought of God. I saw him there kindly...like my own father beckoning but suddenly you were there beside him, Myles, righteous and stern. *(The lights have gone down until there is just her lost in a dim spotlight.)*

I tried to pray but nothing would come. You've stolen my youth and left me barren, you've stolen my gaiety and gave me shame, and when I die I will die unmourned. But I could forgive you swifty, everything except that...seated there at the right hand of God, you had stolen my Christ away from me.

(The set fades into darkness.)

LOW IN THE DARK
by Marina Carr

Set in present day Ireland, this play deals with the difficulties of male-female relationships. Curtains, a young woman hidden behind a set of curtains, finally tells the story at the end of the play she has been struggling to tell all along.

CURTAINS:

So the man and woman joined the millions of men and women at the fork of the road. The millions of men turned to the millions of women and said "I'll not forget you." The millions of women turned and answered, "I'll not forget you either." And so they parted. The men heading north and the women heading south. Before they ever met the man and woman had a dream. It was the same dream, with this difference. The man dreamt he met the woman north by north east. The woman dreamt she met the man south by south west. Long after it was over, the man and woman realized that not only had they never met north by north east or south by south west, much worse, they had never met. And worse still, they never would, they never could, they never can and they never will. *(Theme music comes on, she turns and begins walking off.)* One day the man looked out of his window. "It's time," he said. So he got up on his bicycle and he rode all over the earth and he cycled all over the sea. One evening as he was flying over the highways he saw the woman in his path. "Get out of my road," he yelled, but she would not. "I've two choices," the man said, "I can knock her down or I can stop." He did both. "You," she said, "if you have courage get off your bicycle and come with me."

COGGERERS
by Paul Vincent Carroll

Mrs. Galgoogley, a worn little woman in a library on Easter Monday, 1916, is the custodian of statues of historic insurgents and dead political rebels. The statues speak to her and tell her that her son, Oweneen, will be on the front lines of an impending revolution. She hears gunfire outside the library.

MRS. GALGOOGLEY:

Yous knew this was comin' and yous wouldn't tell me! Yous villains and cut-throats and stinkin' coggers! I that always had the wee word for yous and the wipe of me duster, when the patent leather people passed yous and the high men with big books. And did I not sing for yous the song of the greedy oul' bitch that yous all died for. I know what it is that's up with yous! Yous are jealous of Oweneen and the way his strong arms can fling a hundred o'coal on his shoulder — jealous of the pant of his breath, the cry of his blood and the ring of his heart beats. Yous coggered together to get him into that corner there, to be one of yourselves, yous wicked, jealous, dead oul' vagabonds! But yous'll not get him. My Oweneen has warm blood that he will give not to yous, not to that oul' bitch that wanders O'Connell Street, but to some little soft bit of a girl who will give him back in exchange the livin' life; do yous hear, the livin' life! I'll go out to my Oweneen now, and I will put my woman's body round his, as it was long ago in the beginning. My seven curses on yous and my seven curses on the oul' bitch yous died the death for!

AFTER EASTER
by Anne Devlin

Greta, an Irish woman in her late thirties living in present day England, explains her dream to her newborn baby. Through this she relates her search for identity culminating in a discovery of her mystical Irish roots.

GRETA:

After Easter we came to the place. It was snowing in the forest and very cold into the fifth month. My mother and I were hunting. But because of the cold we couldn't feel anything or find anything to eat. So we sat down by the stream. I looked up and saw it suddenly, a stag, antlered and black, profiled against the sky. It stood on a ridge. This stag was from the cold north. It leapt off the ridge and down into the stream. It leapt through hundreds of years to reach us. And arrived gigantic in the stream. My mother was afraid, but I saw that it was only hungry. I took some berries from my bag and fed the stag from the palm of my hand. The stag's face was frozen and I had to be careful because it wanted to kiss me, and if I had let it, I would have died of cold. But gradually as it ate, its face was transformed and it began to take on human features. And then the thaw set in — I could hear the stream running, and the snow began to melt. I could hear all the water of the forest rushing and it filled my years with a tremendous sound. *(Pause.)* So I got on the stag's back and flew with it to the top of the world. And he took me to the place where the rivers come from, where you come from...and he took me to the place where the rivers come from, where you come from...and this is my own story.

THE QUEEN'S ENEMIES
by Lord Dunsany

The Queen banquets with those who would be her enemies. She has tasted the feast and wine to show that it's not poisoned and now offers the return of land. Soon, however, she will unleash the floodwaters of the Nile and drown all the enemy leaders who have gathered in her trap.

QUEEN:
O feast with me a little longer and make merry, and be my enemies no more. Rhadamandaspes, there is some country eastwards towards Assyria, is there not? — I do not know its name — a country which your dynasty claims of me...

...and for whose sake you are my enemy and your fierce uncle, Prince Zophernes.

I will call my captains to me. I will call them down from their high places and reprove them and bid them give the country back to you that lies eastwards towards Assyria. Only you shall tarry here at the feast and forget you ever were my enemies...forget...

You will not leave me alone then here tonight.

And in the matter of the merchant me that trade amongst the isles, they shall offer spices at *your* feet, not at mine, and then men of the isles shall offer goats to *your* gods.

But you will not leave my banquet and go unfriendly away.

All Ethiopia shall be yours, down to the unknown kingdoms fo the beasts.

Stay then and feast with me. For not to have enemies is the beggar's joy; and I have looked from windows long and long, envying those that go their ways in rags. Stay with me, dukes and princes.

Princes and gentlemen, let us drink to the future. And we, we will drink to the future and to forgetting — to the forgetting of our enemies.

THE FIRST MRS. FRASER
by St. John Ervine

Janet Fraser, an attractive woman in her late forties, speaks with her ex-husband James. He has proposed that she remarry him, in order to save his reputation. It seems his second wife, Elsie, for whom he divorced Janet, has decided to divorce him.

JANET:

Listen, James, I lived with you for twenty years, a devoted and loyal wife. At the end of that time you discarded me...wait, I haven't done yet. I don't mind telling you now, that I felt that my life was finished then. The boys were at school. All the people I knew ceased to have any real relation to me...I suppose you don't realise how much of her life a married woman spends in entertaining her husband's friends and being bored to death by people who don't interest her.

Some of them did, dreadfully, but I had to be civil to them because they were important from a business point of view. You never had much time for my friends, and they gradually dropped out of my life. When the divorce came, I had nobody. I was a very lonely woman. But I'm like you — it takes more than a blow like that to knock me out. I started to make my life again. It was no longer necessary to think all the time of what you wanted to do, and I began to do things that I wouldn't have dreamt of doing when we were married. I joined societies. Some of them bored me, but one or two of them were interesting. I went to concerts. You hate music, don't you? You never would go the the opera with me. Well, I joined a little club that met in a private home to listen to chamber music. I'm rather fond of chamber music...used to take me to the theatre. Oh, but, my dear James, what sort of plays did you take me to? You wouldn't go to anything but musical comedy. You were always too tired in the evening to do anything else. I did all sorts of things and went all sorts of places and made great many friends. I dine with Philip every Tuesday. So you see, James, I've succeeded in making a very pleasant and agreeable life. I'm valued for myself, and not merely as somebody's wife.

CANARIES
by Bernard Farrell

Madalene, twenty-nine, is in love with Fergus, and both are staying at the same modern resort hotel on the Canary Islands. Fergus, a priest who is hiding his profession while on holiday, cannot return Madalene's advances. To appear nonchalant in the face of his spurning her, Madalene engages in promiscuous activity and begins drinking heavily. She lectures the people with whom she has been vacationing about their hypocrisy.

MADALENE: *(To Jane.)* Oh no, darling — the weather should not affect us: not the holiday people. Here we always are happy, always singing. Here, we are *condemned* to sing and be happy — whatever the weather. *(To Tommy.)* Do you remember that tender story about your canary — the one that continued to sing, right to the end?

[Tommy: What?]

MADALENE: Oh, you remember — it used to sing happily — all the time.

[Marie: Is it the one we had? The one that was chirping away when it was really?...]

MADALENE: Yes! Well, in weather like this, I feel like becoming that canary — being happy and carefree, chirping away, not a worry in the world. Singing as I flutter to my room, then carefully locking my cage and then filling that lovely, blue, sunken bath with gushing hot water...and then, slowly, one by one, taking off all my feathers, gently trailing each bit of feathery clothing across the bathroom tiles until I am quite, quite naked....plucked naked. *(Pause.)* Is this upsetting anyone? No?

[Fergus: Listen, Madalene...]

[Tommy: Such a thing to be going on with...]

MADALENE: *(Loudly.)* No! *(Quietly again.)* No, it's not upsetting anyone because I am still happily singing like a canary so no one need worry about me. *(Pause.)* And then, when the bathroom walls and mirrors are coated in steam and everything is as warm and cosy as a...a nest, I pour myself a glass of champagne. And I carry it with me to the steaming bath and then pause, just pause, in my singing to drink a toast to all illusions and to all deceptions.

To toast the illusion that we are not alone — that outside our cages, there must be something — God? Friends? A friend?...to toast the illusion of lovers, spy ships, trust, truth. And then I get into that bath and I shatter that champagne glass on the edge as I shatter all the illusions and all the deceptions — and I take one long, sharp spear of glass, I take it down into the hot steaming water where a tender, victim vein *(Looks at the underside of her wrist.)* waits to be severed...down in the painful, steaming hot water where the heat allows no cutting to be felt at all...where all escape is painless.

LOVERS
by Brian Friel

Mag, a seventeen-year-old living in western Ireland in the 1960s is described as "bubbling with life and inclined to be extreme in her enthusiasms." She has recently discovered that she is pregnant and must marry Joe, the seventeen-year-old father of her child.

MAG:

I can see the boarders out on the tennis courts. They should be studying. And there's a funeral going up High Street; nine cars, and a petrol lorry, and an ambulance. Maybe the deceased was run over by the petrol lorry — the father of a large family — and the driver is paying respects and crying his eyes out. If he doesn't stop blubbering, he'll run over someone else. And the widow is in the ambulance, all in plaster, crippled for life. *(She stakes out a mime of this — both arms and legs cast in awkward shapes.)* And the children are going to be farmed out to cruel aunts with squints and mustaches. Sister Michael has a beard. Joan O'Hara says she shaves with a cut-throat every first Friday and uses an after-shave lotion called Virility. God, nuns are screams if you don't take them seriously. I think I'd rather be a widow than a widower; but I'd rather be a bachelor than a spinster. And I'd rather be deaf than dumb; but I'd rather be dumb than blind. And if I had to choose between lung cancer, a coronary, and multiple sclerosis, I'd take the coronary. Papa's family all died of coronaries, long before they were commonplace. *(She sits up to tell the following piece of family history.)* He had a sister, Nan, who used to sing at the parochial concert every Christmas; and one year, when she was singing "Jerusalem" — you know, just before the chorus, when the piano is panting Huh-huh-huh-huh-huh-huh, she opened her mouth and dropped like a log...Joe, d'you think *(Quoting something she has read:)* my legs have got thick, my body gross, my facial expression passive to dull, and my eyes lack-luster? I hope it's a boy, and it'll be like you — with a great big bursting brain. Or maybe it'll be twins — like me. I wonder what Peter would have been like? Sometimes when she's very ill Mother calls me Peter. If it were going to be twins I'd rather have a boy and a girl than two boys or two girls; but if it were going to be triplets I'd rather have two boys and a girl or two girls and a boy than three boys and three girls. *(Very wisely and directed to JOE.)* And I have a feeling it's going to be premature.

LOVERS
by Brian Friel

Recently engaged, both Mag and Joe are nearly seventeen. They have rented a poorly ventilated house at the edge of a slaughterhouse field. Nearly hallucinatory with the heat, Mag stares out the window and talks to Joe, who isn't listening.

MAG:

I read in a book that there are one million two thousand nuns in the world. Isn't that fierce? Imagine if they were all gathered in one place — on an island, say — and the Chinese navy was let loose at them — cripes, you'd hear the squeals in Tobermore! I have a wicked mind, too. D'you ever think things like that, Joe? I'm sure you don't. I think that women have far more corrupt minds than men, but I think that men are more easily corrupted than women.

Food! — I don't care if I never see another bite ever again. My God, I thought I was going to vomit my guts out this morning! And this could keep up for the next seven months, according to Doctor Watson. The only consolation is that *you're* all right. It would be wild altogether if you were at it too. Sympathetic sickness, they call it. But it's only husbands get it. Maybe you'll get it this day three weeks — the minute we get married — God, wouldn't that be a scream! D'you know what Joan O'Hara told me? That all the time her mother was expecting Oliver Plunket, her father never lifted his head out of the kitchen sink. Isn't it crazy! And for the last three days he lay squealing on the floor like a stuck pig and her mother had to get the police for him in the end. I love this view of Ballymore: the town and the fields and the lake; and the people. When I'm up here and look down on them, I want to run down and hug them all and kiss them. But then when I'm down among them I feel like doing that *(She cocks a snook into JOE's face.)* into their faces. I bet you that's how God feels at times, too. Wouldn't you think so?

Well, I'll tell you something: there are occasions in my life when I know how God feels.

And one of those occasions is now. At this moment God feels... expansive...and beneficent..and philanthropy.

DONNY BOY
by Robin Glendinning

Cahill, nicknamed "the Quartermaster," has ostensibly murdered a British policeman in the name of the Irish Republican Army. He gives the gun to Donny, a mentally handicapped boy in his late teens, to throw into the river so that Cahill can pass through the police patrols. Ma discovers that Donny has not disposed of the weapon and finds it a badge of her son's bravery.

MA:

But tonight Donny boy you were strong, you were bright, tonight the Quartermaster chose you. He knew you could do it, that only you could do it. Oh I've got to hand it to that cute wee bugger. It's no wonder the Brits have never laid a hand on him. He's a sharp one alright. And he chose you! The people of this town call you a fool, Donny. There goes the half-wit, it's a pity he's not all there, he has a wee want, God love him. I can hear them when I'm out with you Donny; oh, they turn their heads away but I can hear them. Laugh, some of them laugh behind their hands, spiteful bitches. Well, sometimes it takes a fool to show the clever ones the way, doesn't it Donny? Sure weren't all our great leaders counted fools once? Wasn't Tone counted a fool, and Emmet, and the Fenians and Pearse? Wasn't Christ counted a fool going to the cross and all the wise ones wagging their heads — look at that bloody fool of a son of a jumped up carpenter now, and his mother giving herself airs all these years, sure isn't that the very way we all said it would end? Well the wise ones of this town will have to laugh on the other sides of their gobs now, won't they? That's Donny Boy they'll say, that's Donny that fooled the Brits with his mask. The Brits took Donny for a fool and Donny fooled them. Donny's one of the boys.

And, oh son, if you're one of the boys I'm one of the mothers. Never fear I'll play a mother's part, proud to laugh or cheer or weep, proud as only an Irish mother can be proud of her son whose hand was soft on her breast and is now brave and strong on the butt of a gun. I'll not grudge you Donny, no I'll not grudge my only son, my only Donny.

Tho' courage be broken and faith decayed,
Tho' slaves of us all have the Saxons made;

Still dark is the rose in its secret place,
And proud mothers yet bear new sons of the race.
No matter what fear or what danger has passed,
The little dark rose shall be red at last,
Oh the little dark rose shall be red at last.
(She goes and picks up the gun.)
Lovely isn't it? The workmanship. Slim, snug, beautifully tooled, precise, direct, no argument, the clean, the shear thing, blessed instrument of fate.

SPREADING THE NEWS
by Lady Gregory

> *Mrs. Fallon, a middle-aged woman, has just returned to a town's fair where nobody has any business but "to be minding one another's business." Her husband, Bartley Fallon, has left to return a hayfork to Jack Smith. This information, spread amongst the townspeople, has been transformed into an account of Bartley murdering Jack with a hayfork.*

MRS. FALLON:

What is it the whole of the town is talking about? And what is it you yourselves are talking about? Is it about my man Bartley Fallon you are talking? Is it lies about him you are telling, saying that he went killing Jack Smith? My grief that ever he came into this place at all!

Let you be sorry for yourselves, and that there may be shame on you forever and at the day of judgment, for the words you are saying and the lies you are telling to take away the character of my poor man, and to take the good name off of him, and to drive him to destruction! That is what you are doing!

I tell you it's too much talk you have, making yourself out to be such a great one, and to be running down every respectable person! A rope, is it? It isn't much of a rope was needed to tie up your own furniture the day you came into Martin Tully's house, and you never bringing as much as a blanket, or a penny, or a suit of clothes with you and I myself bringing seventy pounds and two feather beds. And now you are stiffer than a woman would have a hundred pounds! It is too much talk the whole of you have. A rope is it? I tell you the whole of this town is full of liars and schemers that would hand you up for half a glass of whiskey. People they are you wouldn't believe as much as daylight from without you'd get up to have a look at it yourself. Killing Jack Smith indeed! Where are you at all, Bartley, till I bring you out of this? My nice quiet little man! My decent comrade! He that is as kind and as harmless as an innocent beast of the field! He'll be doing no harm at all if he'll shed the blood of some of you after this day's work! That much would be no harm at all. Bartley! Bartley Fallon! Where are you? Did anyone see Bartley Fallon?

SAYS I, SAYS HE
by Ron Hutchinson

Gathered in a pub in Belfast, a group of friends drink, dance and brag — they are the very image of "Oirishness." Bella, a brash young woman, is the first to call the men on their boasting.

BELLA:
Shall I tell you Jigger's problem? Like his brother. Like the other hero in the family. Scared shitless at the thought of an honest bit of fanny. At the age of nothing and a half he thumbs up the skirt of one of me dolls and finds to his amazement it not the same at the business end as down the front of his wee trousers — Upshot being the sort of chiseller he was — his ma finds him hanging the bog lid up and down on it, trying to chop it off. Which has put a dent in his entire bloody apparatus to this day. You know the truth of it yourself, Maeve. Petey's only got it in the gab and Jigger when he can feel the weight of that thing in his hand. Just strutting their stuff, the two of them, and not a blind bit of notice should be taken of the pair. A couple of pop-eyed lugs who couldn't hold down jobs as doormats if times was straight. It's the likes of yourself who build them up for heroes. Eeejits. A right dopey pair of bookends, both. Now, your man my brother — he's a different case entirely. There's more than a bit of suss behind that piggy eye of his.

STEP-IN-THE-HOLLOW
by Donagh MacDonagh

Molly Nolan, the attractive young housemaid to the Justice of a small town, speaks to the highly principled Sean O'Fenetic. She has just rejected three separate proposals of marriage before Sean's entrance. He is a government inspector who was sent to investigate the local authorities.

MOLLY:

No, lay it gently here, don't be afraid.

Fear is the enemy of every joy.

Sleep now a little sleep. My little man,

My lost small boy, what are you running from?

Why do you hide from life inside a cave

Of office files? Life is here, as warm, and generous as your own mother's bosom.

Sleep here. Be easy. Rest. Here is the safest place

In all God's world for you. The simple things

Of life, as simple as your own four bones

That grew with you since your last moment here,

Are here again. Here you have never left

Though you have run and hidden, taught yourself

That what you wanted most was worst, not best.

Here is the end of every setting out,

The harbour where all ships return

And drop their anchor.

This you must learn again,

To kiss, to bite as gently as a calf,

Caresses softer than a kitten's fur.

And little words as subtle as little spiders,

The whispered words that keep the night awake.

MAEVE
by Edward Martyn

Set at the turn of the century on the grounds of a ruined abbey in County Clare, the play weaves together themes of loss, love, and the healing powers of mysticism. Maeve, a handsome young girl of twenty-three calls on Queen Maeve, a figure from Irish mythology, when her husband dies unexpectedly.

MAEVE:

Listen and I will tell you, Fiona. You have heard Peg Inerny speak of her other life, and of having dwelt in the place of Queen Maeve.

This very night after I had left her upon the mountain I thought I saw her beckoning me in the abbey. I followed her while she went past the round tower to the cairn which now was glowing against a sky that had turned crimson. With a gesture the old woman seemed to open the cairn, and then stood transformed in a curious region of fresh green suffused with saffron light, so that I saw her tall and beautiful and marvellously pale of face, and crowned with a diadem not so golden as her hair. And I heard her say these words in ancient Gaelic: "Last Princess of Eire, thous are a lonely dweller among strange peoples; but I the Geen Maeve have watched thee from thy birth, for thou wert to be the vestal of our country's last beauty. Behold whom they love hath called to life. Mark him well, for already his hour of dissolution hath come." And I looked and saw him who was beauty standing by the round tower. With a feeling of nothingness, I fell upon my knees and bent down to the earth. When I looked again he was not there. Then a company of ancient Celts bore a covered form upon their shoulders; while a choir of rose-crowned boys sang dirges with violet voices of frail, lace-like beauty. And they buried their dead ones by the round tower, and over his grave they raised a great ogham stone. And again I heard the voice of the Queen: "They have buried thy dead beauty, Princess. Thou hast killed him by deserting thy chosen way of life; for there are no more who live for beauty." Then in my desolation I seemed to lose consciousness of all save these last words of the queen: "Yet, Princess, I will come and comfort thee again tonight." And with a start I discovered that I was sitting alone in the moonlight by the round tower. And I looked and looked, but I could not find the great ogham stone that they had raised over my beloved.

Yes, it must have only been a dream, for my beloved is not dead.

THE GUERNICA HOTEL
by Jim Nolan

Grace lives with her mother, a housekeeper at the "Guernica Hotel," a dilapidated seaside boarding house in present-day Ireland. Grace is getting ready to leave for college when her father Joe, whom she's never met, comes to pay a visit.

GRACE:

I used to break in from the balcony window. It was the summer before I went to boarding school. I'd tell Ma I was going for a walk somewhere and then I'd sneak around the side of the house, up the fire escape and in the window. I wasn't being nosey I swear. Just curious. All I did was look around y'know. And read your books. I read them all that summer.

It was a funny feeling being in there. Sort of like walking through a graveyard in the dark — scary and exciting at the same time. There was a photograph on the wall over your bed. Of you and James and Francis and Mrs. Shannon taken on the beach at Seafield. You must been very happy then because the four of you were grinning at the camera.

I loved that room Joe. Your books, the photograph, your clothes — especially your clothes. There was a shirt, a red check shirt on the dressing table. I'd been looking at it all that summer but for some reason I'd never touch it. And then one day I went into the room and I picked up the shirt and I put it on. I don't know why and I know it was silly but I did. That was the day I got caught. (Pause.) It was the only time your mother ever hit me. I didn't mind being hit but the names hurt. And that wasn't the worst of it. The next day, when Francis was out somewhere, Ma and meself saw James and Mrs. Shannon loading all these cardboard boxes into the boot of James' car. There was a kite hanging from one of the boxes and it fell out. That was how I knew it was your stuff. James turned to pick it up but as he turned he saw Ma and me watching them from the window and he left it there. I screamed at Ma to try and stop them but she just began to cry. So we just stood there. We just stood at the dining room window and watched the car driving down the avenue with all those cardboard boxes in the back. Francis was so angry when he found out.

There was a terrible row and after that I don't think he ever spoke to Mrs. Shannon again. I kept the kite. I have it hidden under my bed. Even Ma doesn't know that. You can have it if you want to.

THE PLOUGH AND THE STARS
by Sean O'Casey

During the Easter Rebellion of 1916, Nora, twenty-two, has just returned to her tenement. She has been searching Dublin unsuccessfully for her husband, a commandant in the Irish Citizen Army.

NORA: I can't help thinkin' every shot fired'll be fired at Jack, an' every shot fired at Jack'll be fired at me. What do I care for th' others? I can only think of me own self....An' there's no woman gives a son or a husband to be killed — if they say it, they're lyin', lyin', against God, Nature, an' against themselves!...One blasted hussy at a barricade told me to go home an' not be thryin' to dishearten th' men...That I wasn't worthy to bear a son to a man that was out fightin' for freedom...I clawed at her, an' smashed her in th' face till we were separated... I was pushed down th' street, an' I cursed them — cursed the rebel ruffians an' Volunteers that had dhragged me ravin' mad into th' sthreets to seek me husband!

[Peter: You'll have to have patience, Nora. We all have to put up with twarthers an' tormentors in this world.]

[The Covey: If they were fightin' for anything worthwhile, I wouldn't mind.]

[Fluther: Nothin' derogatory'll happen to Mr. Clitheroe. You'll find, now, in th' finish up it'll be vice versa.]

Oh, I know that wherever he is, he's thinkin' of wantin' to be with me. I know he's longin' to be passin' his hand through me hair, to be caressin' me neck, to fondle me hand an' to feel me kisses clingin' to his mouth...An' he stands wherever he is because he's brave? (*Vehemently.*) No, but because he's a coward, a coward, a coward!

[Mrs. Gogan: Oh, they're not cowards anyway.]

NORA: (*With denunciatory anger.*) I tell you they're afraid to say they're afraid!...Oh, I saw it, I saw it Mrs. Cogan....At th' barricade in North King Street I saw fear glowin' in all their eyes...An' in th' middle o' th' sthreet was somethin' huddled up in a horrible tangled heap...His face was jammed again th' stones, an' his arm was twisted round his back...An' every twist of his body was a cry against th' terrible thing that had happened to him...An' I saw they were afraid to look at it...An' some o' them laughed at me, but th' laugh was a frightened one...An' some o' them shouted at me, but th' shout had in it th' shiver o' fear... I tell you they were afraid, afraid, afraid.

THE SHADOW OF A GUNMAN
by Sean O'Casey

*It is May 1920 in Dublin. Mrs. Grigson, an Irish Protestant around
forty-years-old, has just left her tenement apartment which is being
raided by British Auxiliary soldiers.*

MRS. GRIGSON:
They're turning the place upside-down. Upstairs an' downstairs they're
makin' a litter of everything! I declare to God, it's awful what law-
abidin' people have to put up with. An' they found a pint bottle of
whiskey under Dolphie's pillow, an' they're drinkin' every drop of it
— an' Dolphie'll be like a devil in the mornin' when he finds he has
no curer.

They didn't leave a thing in the kitchen that they didn't flitter about
the floor; the things in the cupboard, all the little odds an' ends that I
keep in the big box, an...

Just to show them the sort of man he was, before they come in,
Dolphie put the big Bible on the table, open at the First Gospel of St.
Peter, second chapter, an' marked the thirteenth to the seventeenth
verse in red ink — you know the passages, Mr. Shields —

"Submit yourselves to every ordinance of man for the Lord's sake:
whether it be to the king, as supreme; or unto governors, as unto them
that are sent by him for the punishment of evildoers, an' for the praise
of them that do well...Love the brotherhood. Fear God. Honour the
King."

An' what do you think they did, Mr. Shields? They caught a hold
of the Bible an' flung it on the floor — imagine that, Mr. Shields —
flingin' the Bible on the floor! Then one of them says to another —
"Jack," says he, "Have you seen the light; is your soul saved?" An' then
they grabbed hold of poor Dolphie, callin' him Mr. Moody an' Mr.
Sankey, an' wanted him to offer up a prayer for the Irish Republic! An'
when they were puttin' me out, there they had the poor man sittin' up
in bed, his hands crossed on his breast, his eyes lookin' up at the
ceilin', an' he singin' a hymn — "We shall meet in the Sweet Bye an'
Bye" — an all the time, Mr. Shields, there they were drinkin' his
whiskey; there's torture for you, an' they all laughin' at poor Dolphie's
terrible sufferins. He always brings a drop home with him — he calls
it his medicine. An' we have a picture over the mantelpiece of King

William crossin' the Boyne, an' do you know what they wanted to make out, Mr. Shields, that it was Robert Emmet, an' the picture of a sacret society!

There's not a bit of me that's not shakin' like a jelly!

BELFRY
by Billy Roche

*Angela, a young married woman, is having an affair with Artie, a
sacristan in a local church in the 1990s. In that church's belfry, they
kiss and cuddle and fall deeply in love.*

ANGELA:

I went up to see my sister Maude this afternoon...I wanted to tell her
about yeh. But I couldn't. It's funny, there was a time when we used
to tell each other everythin'. Until I discovered that I was doin' all the
talkin'. We used to go nearly everywhere together — myself and
Maude — off to all the dances and all. We were mad as hatters, the
pair of us. Well I was anyway! *(She chuckles.)*

We joined the Irish dancin' one time. We used to come out onto
the back of an auld lorry or somewhere and your man'd start up on
the accordian. Bum bum bum bum bum bum. Bum bum bum bum
bum bum bum...All the boys'd gather round and try to look up our
dresses. Meself and Maude used to give them a right eye full I can tell yeh.

Dancin'? No, we weren't. Sure we hardly ever practised or any-
thin'. I just wanted to get up and show off in front of the crowd like
yeh know. I probably should have been a singer in a band or somethin' Artie shouldn't I? When we were young I was forever draggin'
poor Maude down to stand outside Town Hall every Friday night. It
was durin' the Rock 'N' Roll days and we could see them all jivin' inside — the boys in their snazzy suits, the girls in their big dresses and
all. I used to be dyin' to go in there. I'd've loved that now — clackin'
along in me high heel shoes...By the time we were old enough to go
though the whole scene had started to change...Keep away from
Padraic Lacy, me mother said to me when we were goin' off to our
very first dance. Why? says I. Never mind why, says she. Just keep
away from him that's all. Padraic Lacy had a car and there was a ru-
mour goin' around that he had slipped a girl a Mickey Finn one night
after a dance and while she was drowsy he put his hand up her skirt.
He was one of the first boys I ever went out with. I thought he was a
right creep. He started to cry when I told him I didn't want to see him
again. Maude was lookin' for a prince or some sort of a sheik to whisk
her off to God knows where. She was goin' out with this fella from
Tuam who came to town to work in the bank. A real good-lookin' fella

with sultry eyes. Maude dropped him like a hot brick when she found out that his Da was a plasterer. She was a real snob. She married a guard in the end and went off to live in Suburbia...I never really wanted all the things that other people seem to long for Artie yeh know. Maybe that's why I got them hah?...Donal is still down in the dumps over that auld handball match. The young fella ran rings around him I heard. He won't go out nor nothin' now. He just mopes around the house all day drinkin' mugs of tay. I think he feels it's an end of an era or somethin'. And maybe he's right.

BELFRY
by Billy Roche

Angela, a young married woman living in small town Ireland, is having an affair with Artie O'Leary, a timid church mouse who leads an otherwise lonely existence as sacristan of the local Catholic chapel.

ANGELA:
The heart's its own boss Artie I think. People can give their love away as freely as they want but not the heart. The heart's its own boss boy. *(Artie puts the letter away.)*

I have a photo at home yeh know that keeps turnin' up to kind of haunt me all the time. I'll find it in a drawer or somewhere or down in the end of my handbag when I'm rootin' around for my keys. No idea how it got there!...It was taken on the steps of White's Hotel. Donal's mother and father's fiftieth anniversary it was. We had a bit of a do for them. All the lads came home from England and all for it. This was supposed to be a picture of just the immediate family so I stepped back into the hotel doorway out of the way. It had been snowin' and the steps leadin' up to the hotel were still covered in slush. I think the photographer must have had a few drinks in him or somethin' because when it came out you could see me as clear as day standin' in the background. I looked like an orphan standin' there in the cold. Everybody laughed when they saw it. It was as if I didn't belong in Donal's life at all. You'd swear I was trying' to sneak my way into it or somethin'. Or out of it, whichever the case may be. It's a great photograph though. I'm not coddin' yeh, you can nearly hear them all laughin' in it...

(She chuckles and goes behind the raised lid of the basket, out of sight.)

Our Maude says that there's only two real choices open to people in life yeh know. Whether to tap the good side of them or the bad side. If yeh tap the good side then all you'll see is the good in people and the good in everything and you'll be happy. If yeh tap the bad side of yeh then you'll be devious and snakey and bad and you'll never be really contented. Everytime I look at that photograph I keep thinkin' how contented they all look and I keep wonderin' why I'm not in there with them...*(She emerges, wearing only altar boys's surplus.)* Do yeh think I've tapped the bad side of me Artie?

IN THE SHADOW OF THE GLEN
by John Millington Synge

Nora Burke, a married but excruciatingly lonely middle-aged woman, speaks to Michael, a young shepherd, while her husband lies next to them pretending to be dead. A tramp wandering through the dark and isolated area has stopped to spend the night away from the pounding rain outside.

NORA:

It's a bad night, and a wild night, Michael Dara, and isn't it a great while I am at the foot of the back hills, sitting up here boiling food for himself, and food for the brood sow, and baking a cake when the night falls? *(She puts the money listlessly in little piles on the table.)* Isn't it a long while I am sitting here in the winter and the summer, and the fine spring, with the young growing behind me and the old passing, saying to myself one time to look on Mary Brien, who wasn't that height and I a fine girl growing up, and there she is now with two children, and another coming on her in three months or four.

And saying to myself another time, to look on Peggy Cavanagh, who had the lightest hand at milking a cow that wouldn't be easy, or turning a cake, and there she is now walking round on the roads, or sitting in a dirty old house, with no teeth in her mouth, and no sense, and no more hair than you'd see on a bit of hill and they after burning the furze from it.

Why would I marry you, Mike Dara? You'll be getting old and I'll be getting old, and in a little while, I'm telling you, you'll be sitting up in your bed — the way himself was sitting — with a shake in your face, and your teeth falling, and the white hair sticking out round you like an old bush where sleep do be leaping a gap.

It's a pitiful thing to be getting old, but it's a queer thing surely. It's a queer thing to see an old man sitting up there in his bed with no teeth in him, and a rough word in his mouth, and his chin the way it would take the bark from the edge of an oak board you'd have building a door...God forgive me, Michael Dara, we'll all be getting old, but it's a queer thing surely.

THE TINKER'S WEDDING
by John Millington Synge

Mary Byrne, an old woman, has just returned to her son Michael, a poor tinker with whom she travels, after a night of drinking. She is speaking to Sarah, a destitute young woman who, desperately wanting to be married, has convinced a priest to wed her and Michael.

MARY:

My singing voice is gone for this night, Sarah Casey. *(She lights her pipe.)* But if it's flighty you are itself, you're a grand, handsome woman, the glory of tinkers, the pride of Wicklow, the Beauty of Ballinacree. I wouldn't have you lying down and you lonesome to sleep this night in a dark ditch when the spring is coming in the trees; so let you sit down there by the big bough, and I'll be telling you the finest story there by the big bough, and I'll be telling you the finest story you'd hear any place from Dundalk to Ballinacree, with great queens in it, making themselves matches from the start to the end, and they with shiny silks on them the length of the day, and white shifts for the night.

Don't mind him, Sarah Casey. Sit down now, and I'll be telling you a story would be fit to tell a woman the like of you in the springtime of the year.

Where is it you're going? Let you walk back here, and not be leaving me lonesome when the night is fine.

And it's leaving me lone you are? Come back here, Sarah Casey. Come back here, I'm saying; or if it's off you must go, leave me the two little coppers you have, the way I can walk up in a short while, and get another pint for my sleep.

It's gone they are and I with my feet that weak under me you'd knock me down with a rush; and my head with a noise in it the like of what you'd hear in a stream and it running between two rocks and rain falling. What good am I this night, God help me? What good are the grand stories I have when it's few would listen to an old woman, few but a girl maybe would be in great fear the first time her hour was come, or a little child wouldn't be sleeping with the hunger on a cold night? Maybe the two of them have a good right to be walking out the little short while they'd be young; but if they have itself they'll not keep Mary Byrne from her full pint when the night's fine, and there's a dry moon in the sky. Jemmy Neill's a decent lad; and he'll give me a good drop for the can; and maybe if I keep near the peelers tomorrow for the first bit of the fair, herself won't strike me at all; and if she does itself, what's a little stroke on your head beside sitting lonesome on a fine night, hearing the dogs barking, and the bats squeaking, and you saying over, it's a short while only till you die.

TWENTY-SEVEN MONOLOGUES
FOR MEN

ENDGAME
by Samuel Beckett

Nagg, a sixty-year-old man whose health is failing, lives inside a garbage can. In this monologue he struggles to perform his favorite comic story for his companion Nell.

NAGG:
Let me tell it again.
(Raconteur's voice.)
An Englishman, needing a pair of striped trousers in a hurry for the New Year festivities, goes to his tailor who takes his measurements.
(Tailor's voice.)
"That's the lot, come back in four days, I'll have it ready."
Good. Four days later.
(Tailor's voice.)
"So sorry, come back in a week, I've made a mess of the seat."
Good, that's all right, a neat seat can be very ticklish. A week later.
(Tailor's voice.)
"Frightfully sorry, come back in ten days, I've made a hash of the crotch." Good, can't be helped, a snug crotch is always a teaser. Ten days later.
(Tailor's voice.)
"Dreadfully sorry, come back in a fortnight, I've made a balls of the fly." Good at a pinch, a smart fly is a stiff proposition.
(Pause. Normal voice.)
I never told it worse.
(Pause. Gloomy.)
I tell this story worse and worse.
(Pause. Raconteur's voice.)
Well, to make it short, the bluebells are blowing and he ballockses the button holes.
(Customer's voice.)
"God damn you to hell, Sir, no, it's indecent, there are limits! In six days, do you hear me, six days, God made the world. Yes Sir, no less Sir, the WORLD! And you are not bloody well capable of making me a pair of trousers in three months!"
(Tailor's voice, scandalized.)
"But my dear Sir, my dear Sir, look —

(Disdainful gesture, disgustedly.)
—at the world—
(Pause.)
and look —
(Loving gesture, proudly.)
—at my TROUSERS!"
(Pause. He looks at Nell who has remained impassive, her eyes unseeing, breaks into a high forced laugh, cuts it short, pokes his head towards Nell, launches his laugh again.)

RICHARD'S CORK LEG
by Brendan Behan

*In a church cemetary in Dublin, Cronin, an Irish nationalist posing
as a blind man, tries his hand at seducing young Deidre.*

CRONIN:

(Sitting, addressing audience.) My wife tries to cheer me up by saying
that girls like me — that she loves me. But then she is my wife. I mean,
I don't mean that she just loves me because a wife is supposed to love
her husband. Ah no! My wife is a very, very, exceptional person, and
she is very kind to everyone, and particularly to me.

But I'll tell you something for nothing. There's a lot of nonsense
given out by the English and Americans about our attitude to women.
They say it just to flatter themselves. Some old Jesuit in America attacks
the Irish for not screwing early and often enough. A hundred years ago
screwing and having kids was out of fashion and Paddy was being
lambasted because he got married too soon, and had too many kids.
It's like saying all Jews are capitalists because Rothschild is a capital-
ist, and all Jews are Reds because Karl Marx was a Jew — if they don't
get you one way they get you another. If they don't get you by the
beard, they get you by the balls.

The English and Americans dislike only *some* Irish — the same
Irish that the Irish themselves detest, Irish writers — the ones who
think. But then they hate their own people who think. I just like to
think, and in this city I'm hated and despised. They give me beer, because I can say things that I remember from my thoughts — not everything, because, by Jesus, they'd crucify you, and you have to remember that when you're drunk, but some things, enough to flatter them.

The great majority of Irish people believe that if you become a
priest or a nun, you've a better chance of going to heaven. If it's a
virtue to meditate in a monastery and get food and shelter for doing it
— why then isn't it a virtue outside. I'm a lay contemplative — that's
what I am.

RICHARD'S CORK LEG
by Brendan Behan

A group of bawds have gathered in a Dublin cemetary to mourn the death of one of their colleagues. Cronin, an Irish nationalist and lover of wine and women, has disguised himself as a blind man to gain sympathy and favors from the prostitutes.

CRONIN:

(He sings:)

> 'Twas during my spasm, I had my orgasm,
> Coitus interruptitus,
> Old Kinsey, his report and all
> Old Kinsey, his report and all.

Kinsey is like Shaw. Shaw made our great grandparents and our grandparents so Shavian that they criticized him in the light of what he taught them to accept as ordinary common sense. It's the same with Kinsey. Kinsey! He was reassuring to everyone. When he announced for instance that ninety per cent of males had masturbated in their youth. You missed a damned good thing! But what can scientists tell you about seduction. They go round parked cars with tape recorders. People don't always use the same ploy. Just now, I am the Cynical European Intellectual. If you shout at a girl... "You have lovely eyes?" that was my grandfather's line. He was an actor and theatre manager. In a play called *A Royal Divorce* he acted Talleyrand, and seduced Josephine on the stage at the Queen's Theatre, Dublin. It must have been a Passion Play. Talking about the Passion Play, my grandfather used to leave the theatre dark during Holy Week. One year he hadn't been doing so well and couldn't really afford to close. All the other theatres were owned by Presbyterians and Jews. If he opened everyone would say the Presbyterians and Jews had more respect for Holy Week than he did. But anyway, his brilliant son came to him and said, "Father I know what we'll do." "Do you now, Socrates," said my grandfather, for he called his son Socrates, and his daughter Sappho, because they acted together as husband and wife in the play called *When Greek Meets Greek* — she divorces him for being indifferent — real classical drama. "Well, what is it, Socrates?" "We'll put on a Passion Play for Holy Week." "Did you want to get us burned at the stake? or summonsed or something." "You must not know what a Passion Play is," said my Uncle Socrates. "I most certainly do," said my granda. "It's all the Paris stuff. Wasn't I acting in one of those A la Francay leg shows in the Windmill Theatre in London." "It's not that kind of a Passion Play," said my Uncle Socrates, "it's about the passion of Our Lord." "The passion of Our Who?" said my grandfather in horror. "Now look here, Sock, my son, I've been forty years in show business, but I will not stand for a blasphemy of that nature apart from the fact that it would be illegal not to say unprofitable." "Arrah, you don't know what you are talking about — they have it out in Germany, in Obberammergau and get thousands of people from all over the world to go and pay into it." They do to this very day. So my Uncle Socrates explains to my granda about the Passion Play and he says, "That's great — we'll do great business with matinees for convents and colleges — only one thing." "What's that?" asks my Uncle Socrates. "What'll we do with the Queen's Moonbeams?" These were the chorus girls. They were usually employed in dance numbers that you would not perform for convents or colleges. "Ph, that's all right," said Uncle Socrates, "they will dance in very little." "Well," said my grandfather, "they wear so little now, it's only the Grace of God they're not all dead from pneumonia, but can we get away with it?" "Certainly," says my Uncle Socrates. "Isn't it a class of a religious sermon against the Pharisees that crucified Christ." "Satisfyingly dramatic. Well, O.K.," says my grandfather. "But you won't forget to put in a plug for me ould friend Wille Rouke, the Baker, he puts his ad on the Fire Curtain?" "Rourke, the Baker, will have his plug," said my uncle, "and in a place in the drama where all shall know it." And so he had, for at the Last Supper, when Saint Peter passes Our Lord the wine and bread, he says, "Take this and eat — it's Rourke's bread, fresh and crusty."

Well there you are. You know all about me, and I know nothing about you I don't even know if you are a virgin. Well, if you are not it's a sin against God, and if you are it's a sin against man. The sin against man is more important because we see God so seldom. However, if I can remedy the other. "If any nice girls shall come among you, I will fix them up." There there. All this old chat of mine is a means of covering my shyness. We'll talk lovingly when you get to know me better.

DESIGN FOR A HEADSTONE
by Seamus Byrne

Conor, a middle-aged inmate in an Irish prison, has been sentenced to criminal confinement instead of the "political treatment" to which he is entitled. His cellmates rally to his cause with threats of a hunger strike.

CONOR:

All rights lads. I'm not going to talk about hunger strike. But something that concerns all of you — I'll talk about solitary instead. Tommy, there, knows a great deal more about it than I do: that's where he learnt to make rings. But *some* of you may find what *I* have to say helpful. Solitary *can* be undermining, over a long period. No books, no papers. Sometimes, not even a rosary beads. Yes, you can do a lot of things with a beads, besides just pray. Fiddle with them — feel them — get to recognize, by touch alone, a flaw in a single bead. Four white walls to four black walls, changing to four white walls again. Dreary enough! Play tricks with the light that streams down from the cell window — project an image onto the wall, and wait for the shadowy bars to form again against the white. Trace the veins in the back of your hand. Or study, the millionth time, the Venetian red door, unsmiling as a sulky child. Yes, it *can* be undermining; but it need not be at all. Set out for a walk from your home place, as I often did, in my mind's eye; though I never got very far on the walk, for I stopped and chatted with people I knew, and with people I didn't even like; for I really didn't know them at all till I met them again — in solitary. And those — the ones I thought I knew well — met them again — knew them afresh — my father — and my mother. No. Solitary need not be a loss; it wasn't for me: nor will it be for you. Some of you will think this strange — but when I heard of this new threat — solitary! — again! — something leapt inside me, that was very like a welcome. That's all, lads — except, good luck!

THE GLITTERING GATE
by Lord Dunsany

Jim and Bill, two thieves, stand outside the pearly gates of heaven. Jim, an older man who has been shot in the head, has been there for some time and has given up all hope of entering paradise. Bill, recently dead and with a spiral lockpick in hand, is determined to open the gates.

BILL:

This isn't a safe, Jim, this is Heaven. There'll be the old saints with their halos shining and flickering, like windows o' wintry nights. And angels thick as swallows along a cottage roof the day before they go. And orchards full of apples as far as you can see, and the rivers of Tigris and Euphrates, so the Bible says; and a city of gold, for those that care for cities, all full of precious stones; but I'm a bit tired of cities and precious stones. I'll go out into the fields where the orchards are, by the Tigris and the Euphrates. I shouldn't be surprised if my old mother was there. She never cared much for the way I earned my livelihood, but she was a good mother to me. I don't know if they want a good mother in there who would be kind to the angels and sit and smile at them when they sang and soothe them if they were cross. If they let all the good ones in she'll be there all right. Jim! They won't have brought me up against her, will they? That's not fair evidence, Jim.

If there's a glass of beer to be got in Heaven, or a dish of tripe and onions, or a pipe of 'bacca she'll have them for me when I come to her. She used to know my ways wonderful; and what I liked. And she used to know when to expect me almost anywhere. I used to climb in through the window at any hour and she always knew it was me. She'll know it's me at the door now, Jim. It will be all a blaze of light, and I'll hardly know it's her till I get used to it...But I'll know here among a million angels. There weren't none like her on Earth and there won't be none like her in Heaven...Jim! I'm through, Jim! One more turn, and old Nut Cracker's done it! It's giving! It's giving! I know the feel of it. *Jim!*

JOHN FERGUSON
by St. John Ervine

In the late 1800s, James Caesar, a prosperous grocer in his midthirties, has just found out that Hannah Ferguson has decided that she cannot marry him. She had agreed to it as a way of saving her family's farm from foreclosure. Here James speaks with Hannah's family.

JAMES CAESAR: *(Fiercely.)* I want her, don't I? What does it matter to me whether she wants me or not so long as I'm married to her? My heart's hungry for her! Don't I know rightly she doesn't want me? But what does that matter to me? I've loved her since she was a wee child, and I'd be happy with her if she was never to give me a kind look. Many and many a time, when the shop was closed, I went and sat out there in the fields and imagined her and me married together and living happy, us with two or three wee children, and them growing up fine and strong. I could see her them times walking about in a fine silk dress, and looking grand in it, and all the neighbours nudging each other and saying the fine woman she was and how well we must be getting on in the world for her to be able to dress herself that nice! I could hardly bear it when I used to meet her afterwards, and her hadn't hardly a civil word for me; but I couldn't keep out of her way for all that; and many's a time I run quick and dodged round corners so's I should meet her again and have the pleasure of looking at her. When she said she'd have me, I could feel big Jumps rolling off me, and I was light-hearted and happy for all I knew she was only consenting to have me to save your farm, John. I had my heart's desire, and I never so felt like a man before!...And now!...
(He rests his head on table and begins to sob.)

[Sarah Ferguson: I can't bear to see a man crying! Quit, Jimmy, son. It'll mebbe be all right in the end. Don't disturb yourself so much, man!]

[Andrew Ferguson: There's no sense in going on that way!]

[John Ferguson: Don't speak to him, Andrew! Leave the man to his grief!]

JAMES CAESAR: *(Looking up, addressing Andrew.)* I know rightly I'm making a poor show of myself, but I can't help it. Wouldn't anybody that's had the life that I've had do the same as me? You're right and fine, Andrew, full of your talk, but wait till you've had to bear what I have, and you'll see then what you'll do when something good that you've longed for all your life comes to you and then is taken from you. *(He rises from the table, trying to recover himself and speak in an ordinary voice.)* I'm sorry I bothered you all! I'll not trouble you with my company any longer. It'll be better for me to be going nor to be here when she comes back.

LOVERS
by Brian Friel

Joe and Mag, a married couple in their late teens, have just leased their first apartment, which is located at the edge of a slaughterhouse.

JOE:

I signed the lease yesterday evening.

Old Kerrigan was so busy working he wouldn't take time off to go into the office; so we put the document on the back of a cow that was about to be shot and that's where we signed it. Cockeyed old miser!

I'm telling you. And crazy, too. In a big rubber apron and him dripping with blood. And cows and sheep and bullocks dropping dead all around him.

"Drive him up there! Another beast. C'mon! C'mon! I haven't all day. And what's bothering you, young Brennan? Steady, there. Steady! Bang! Bang! Drag it away! Slit its throat! Slice it open! Skin it!"

Another beast! Get a move on! What am I paying you fellas for? You told me about the flat, Mr. Kerrigan. "Steady-bang! Bang! Damnit, I nearly missed—bang!— that's it. Drag him off. What are you saying, young Brennan? The lease? Oh, the lease! Oh, aye. Here we are." *(Joe produces an imaginary document from his hip pocket.)* "Best flat in town. Hell, it's all blood now." *(Joe wipes the imaginary document on his leg.)* "Come on! Another animal! There's a fine beast for you, young Brennan! Look at those shanks! Bang! Bang! Never knew what hit him! I sign here, son, don't I?" *(Joe pretends to write: but the pen does not work and he flings it away.)* "Hell, that doesn't write."

PHILADELPHIA, HERE I COME!
by Brian Friel

Private and Public are two sides of the same man, Gar O'Donnell, twenty-five. He is planning to go to Philadelphia to work in a hotel to escape the mundane routine of his life in Ireland. Here he addresses his father, S.B. O'Donnell, whom he refers to as Screwballs.

PRIVATE:

Ah! That's what we were waiting for: complete informality; total relaxation between inmates. Now we can carry on. Screwballs. I'm addressing you, Screwballs.

Thank you.

Screwballs, we've eaten together like this for the past twenty-odd years, and never once in all that time have you made as much as one unpredictable remark. Now, even though you refuse to acknowledge the fact, Screwballs, I'm leaving you forever. I'm going to Philadelphia, to work in an hotel. And you know why I'm going, Screwballs, don't you. Because I'm twenty-five, and you treat me as if I were five — I can't order even a dozen loaves without getting your permission. Because you pay me less than you pay Madge. But worse, far worse than that, Screwballs, because — *we embarrass one another.* If one of us were to say, "You're looking tired" or "That's a bad cough you have," the other would fall over backways with embarrassment. So tonight d'you know what I want you to do? I want you to make one unpredictable remark, and even though I'll still be on that plane tomorrow morning, I'll have doubts: Maybe I should have stuck it out; maybe the old codger did have feelings; maybe I have maligned the old bastard. So now, Screwballs, say..."Once upon a time a rainbow ended in our garden"...say, "I like to walk across the White Strand when there's a misty rain falling"...say "Gar, son —" say, "Gar, you bugger you, why don't you stick it out here for me for it's not such a bad aul bugger of a place." Go on. Say it! Say it! Say it!

TRANSLATIONS
by Brian Friel

1833. Owen and Yolland, two young soldiers, have been charged with Anglicizing the Gaelic names of towns across Ireland for a map company. This begins to weigh strangely on Owen's conscience.

OWEN:

Back to the romance again. All right! Fine! Fine! Look where we've got to. We've come to this crossroads. Come here and look at it, man! Look at it! And we call that crossroads Tobair Vree. And why do we call it Tobair Vree? I'll tell you why. Tobair means a well. But what does Vree mean? It's a corruption of Brian — *(Gaelic pronuciation.)* Brian— an erosion of Tobair Bhriain. Because a hundred — and — fifty years ago there used to be a well there, not at the crossroads, mind you — that would be too simple — but in a field close to the crossroads. And an old man called Brian, whose face was disfigured by an enormous growth, got it into his head that the water in that well was blessed; and every day for seven months he went there and bathed his face in it. But the growth didn't go away; and one morning Brian was found drowned in that well. And ever since that crossroads is known as Tobair Vree — even though that well has long since dried up. I know the story because my grandfather told it to me. But ask Doalty — or Maire — or Bridget — even my father — even Manus — why it's called Tobair Vree; and do you think they'll know? I know they don't know. So the question I put to you, Lieutenant, is this: what do we do with a name like that? Do we scrap Tobair Vree altogether and call it — what? — The Cross? Crossroads? Or do we keep piety with a man long dead, long forgotten, his name "eroded" beyond recognition, whose trivial little story nobody in the parish remembers?

GRANIA
by Lady Gregory

Living in Ireland in a far-off time, Finn is a respected General who has been promised the hand of the beautiful Princess Grania. But on the eve of their wedding day, Grania falls in love with Finn's heretofore reliable friend and confidant, Diarmuid. The two betray Finn by eloping, setting off a seven year battle which sends the lovers into exile.

FINN: But you will listen, and you will give heed to it. You came of your own free will to Almhuin to be my wife. And my heart went out to you there and then, and I thought there would be the one house between us, and that it was my child I would see reared on your knee. And that was known to every one of my people and of my armies, and you were willing it should be known. And after that, was it a little thing that all Ireland could laugh at the story that I, Finn, was so spent, and withered, and loathsome in a woman's eyes, that she would not stop with me in a life that was full and easy, but ran out from me to travel the roads, the same as any beggar having seven bags. And I am not like a man of the mean people, that can hide his grief and his heart-break, bringing it to some district where he is not known, but I must live under that wrong and that insult in full sight of all, and among mockery and malicious whisperings in the mouth of those maybe that are shouting me!

[Grania: I have a great wrong done to you, surely, but it brings me no nearer to you now. And our life is settled, and let us each go our own course.]

FINN: Is it not a great wonder the candle you lighted not to have been quenched in all that time? But the light in your grey eyes is my desire for ever, and I am pulled here and there over hills and through hollows. For my life was as if cut in two halves on that night that put me to and fro; and the half that was full and flowing was put behind me, and it has been all on the ebb since then. But you and I together could have changed the world entirely, and put a curb upon the spring-tide, and bound the seven elements with our strength. And now, that is not the way I am, but dragging there and hither, my feet wounded with thorns, the tracks of tears down my cheeks; not taking rest on the brink of any thick wood, because you yourself might be in it, and not stopping on the near side of any lake or inver because you might be on the far side; as wakeful as a herd in lambing time, my companions stealing away from me, being tired with the one corn-crake cry upon my lips always, that is, Grania. And it is no wonder the people to hate you, and but for dread of me they would many a time have killed you.

HANRAHAN'S OATH
by Lady Gregory

*Hanrahan, a young man living before the Irish potato famine, has er-
roneously informed upon a friend. The friend is now in jail due to
Hanrahan's action. Now repentant, Hanrahan has sworn an oath of
silence so that he may avoid all possibility of future sin. An old man,
Coey, has just failed at making small talk with Hanrahan, who has
chased him away with a rock.*

HANRAHAN:

Ah, what is it ails you? That you may never be better this side of
Christmas...What am I doing? Is it speaking in spite of myself I am?
What at all can I do! I to speak, I am breaking my oath; and I not to
speak, I have the world terrified. *(Sits down dejectedly, then starts.)*
What is that? A thorn that ran into me...a whitethorn bush...It is Heaven
put it in my way. There is no sin or no harm to be talking with a bush,
that is a fashion among poets. Oh, my little bush, it is a saint I am out
and out! It is a man without blame I will be from this time! To go
through the whole gamut of the heat and of the frost with no person
to be annoying me till I get a fit of talk and be letting out wicked
words, that is surely the road will reach to Paradise. It is a right plan
I made and a right penance I put on myself. As I converse now with
yourself, the same as with a living person, so every living person I may
hold talk with, and my penance ended, I will think them to be as
harmless as a little whitethorn bush. It is a holy life I will follow, and
not be annoyed with the humans of the world that do be prattling and
prating, carrying mischief here and there, lavish in tale-bearing and
talk! It is a great sin from God Almighty to be ballyragging and drawing scandal on one another risking quarrels and rows! I declare to honest goodness the coneys and the hares are ahead of most Christians on
the road to heaven, where they have not the power to curse and
damn, or to do mischief through flatteries and chatterings and coax-
ings and jestings and jokings and riddles and fables and fancies and
vanities, and backbitings and mockeries and mumblings and grum-
blings and treacheries and false reports! It is free I am now from the
screechings and vain jabberings of the world, in this holy quiet place
that is all one nearly with the blessed silence of heaven!

EEJITS
by Ron Hutchinson

Daly, a blind, middle-aged man, speaks of his aggressive friends. They are his ex-band musicians who have go on without him. He has become a sort of hanger-on who follows them around to hear their music and to drink.

DALY:
Them *are* boys, them are.

Roaring boys.

Steam-shovels; pile-drivers; hard to love; great lads.

Buckaroos.

The left hand of hell in a fight; not Englishmen; love a row; love a sinner.

(Wipes nose with back of hand.) That way meself, before the lights went out.

Loved a row. Give you a quid to fight with you; drink till the morning like a brother with you when it was over.

(Shakes head.) Me and that old Gribben there — a team. Two-handed. Not a pub between here and Goldhawk Road we haven't been marked in; sing you a song or punch you in the gob, take your pick; punch you in the gob, pick you off the floor, drink with you like a brother; take your pick, what's it to be — punch in the gob, just a touch with the chairleg, stick your head through the bog window; or sing you a song?

(Pause.)

Fighting. That's the meat for me. Fighting and singing and fighting and singing.

That's man's work.

Me and that old Gribben —

(*Shakes head, remembering.*)

Every bar between here and...

(*Shakes head.*)

What a bloody waste of time.

(*Feels his way to bar and feels drink. Opens bottle and sups, propped on bar.*)

EEJITS
by Ron Hutchinson

In an empty nightclub, Parnell, an aging drummer for a second-rate band, dramatically informs Mathewson why he sometimes performs while drunk.

PARNELL:
Yeah.

(Shrugs.)

You not been in the business, you wouldn't know...

(Lights dim.)

Nothing they like bettern to see a fella taking a few pints—

(Sways and thickens speech.)

Losing his heels—

(Totters back as if drunk.)

Fighting his own coat off his back —

Off comes the old wife — strangler —

(Untidily pulls tie off and throw it on floor.)

Will all of yous —

(Points out at audience, spot on him only.)

will all of yous who know the next chorus shut your bloody gobs. We're the ones getting paid for this...

Can I ask our soprano here, Megan for the note — thanks —

(Blows raspberry.)

Ta.
You never noticed that about singers?

Fart like a Co-op horse.

Never notice?

Something to do with the cheeks, I suppose,

I don't know —

Let's have it again, love —

(Raspberry again.)

That's the one. You think that's enough to shift a platoon of camel-drivers off the latrines in fear for their lives, you ought to hear her in the bath.

(Drinks from bottle.)

Anyway folks, here we go —

(Raspberry again.)

There's your note and —
Oh — by the way. Been asked to tell you — be doing our usual spot the Stanley Arms Monday nights this winter — so there's somewhere else you'll have to cross off your list —

(Looks at scrappy piece of paper.)

Wednesday we're playing upstairs, week about in the Queer's Pub in Albemarle Terrace, come one come all —

Thursday —

Hang on.

(Pretends to pluck eyeballs out and transfer them.)

Sorry about that. Came out in a rush.

Thursday Gribben here lays on a treat in store for all music lovers in the district — he gives the band the night off —

And over the weekend, if you see large crowds of people streaming out pubs and clubs here and there you'll know someone's been daft enough to give us a booking.

(Shoves paper in back pocket and looks round.)

Well then, they're all out the piss-house and now —
Oh — hang on —

(Takes another piece of paper.)

Another message.

Connor says —

(Squints at paper.)

Hang on. Haven't got me reading eyes in.

(Pretends to pluck eyes out, put them in pocket and take other out and fit them.)

Better.
Connor says he'd like to apologise to the young girl he inadvertently exposed himself to on the stairs just now.

He wouldn't like her to think he makes it a practise to go urinating up the sides of public staircases. No. In actual fact he was having a wank so set your mind at rest.

(Looks round.)

All ready, then?

(Takes drink and spills it down shirt.)

Would you look at that?

(Slaps stain with back of hand.)

Clean on last December.

Or was it October?

Anyway —

There was these two nuns in the bath and one says to the other where's the soap? and the other says yes doesn't it?

Here we go then —

By the way, me brother was supposed to be playing the Anatolian bag-pipes this number but there's no such thing so you'll have to put up with the usual noise the five of us make —

One two, one two —

(Pause.)

Now don't call out, I'll remember in a minute.

(Takes another drink.)

Mind I was telling you last time about me brother? Was going to take up tap-dancing? Wasn't doing too bad at it either, only he kept falling in the sink.

Wears the soap, get it?

(Shrugs.)

Please yourselves, we got your money anyway...

Here we go then, one two three — four —

(Stamps foot and holds hand up as lights come up. Holds it a moment.)

Yeah.

See?

(Sniffs and comes off stage, picking up tie.)

They love it. Paddy, see. Few beers.

Expect it.

And the secret of the business is give them...no surprises.

THE MOON IN THE YELLOW RIVER
by Denis Johnston

In late September 1927, George, a "well-seasoned and weather-beaten old salt," has just completed a tiny model of a ship in a bottle. A girl of thirteen, Blanaid, has been observing him with keen interest.

GEORGE:

Well, kid, we got into Cape Town, and the Captain he drew a chalk line across the deck abaft the fiddley door and he said to me: "Quartermaster," he said, "the Doctor and I are going ashore on important business. See that none of those women cross that line." "Ay, ay, sir," said I. So off he and the Doctor went in a hansom cab.

Women on board: hundred and thirty-two. All cooks and housemaids. Government emigrants for Sydney. Never such a cargo known before, my dear.

Well, I sat at the end of the gangway chatting with the little brown-eyed one, and by and by along comes the one called Scotch Annie, at the head of twenty-five whopping great females. "Annie," said I, "you can't go ashore. Captain's orders." "George," said Annie, "we like you. You're a good sort. And me and these girls don't want to have to sock you one on the jaw." "OK, Annie," said I, "I like you too." And with that up the gangway and ashore they went and the whole hundred and thirty-two after them. All but the little brown-eyed one who stayed chatting with me.

About an hour later up drives a hansom cab at the gallop with the Captain and the Doctor hanging out and shouting bloody murder. "Quartermaster," yells the Captain, "what the hell does this mean? Whole town's had to close down. Those damn women are everywhere." And then drives up another hansom cab with two policemen and one cook in it. "Emigrant from the *Triumph,* sir." Shove her on board. Salute. Off. Another hansom cab. Two more policemen. Two housemaids. "Emigrants from the *Triumph,* sir." Shove 'em on board. Salute. Off. All night. Hansom cabs. Policemen. Cooks and housemaids. Shove 'em on board. Salute. Off. Sailed next morning twenty-nine short. Next year the Boer War.

THE OLD LADY SAYS "NO!"
by Denis Johnston

Older man and younger man are playing cards. They are having a heated disagreement about Ireland's political future.

YOUNGER MAN:

What man says we're not a Free State? I say it, ye drunken bastard! I've been up to hell all right, never fear. I went down into hell shouting "Up the living Republic," and I came out of hell still shouting, "Up the living Republic." Do you hear me? "Up the Republic!"

Every day and every night while you were lying on your back snoring, wasn't I out in the streets shouting "Up the living Republic?"

Every morning and every night while you were sitting in the old snug, wasn't I out on the hills shouting "Up the living Republic?"

Every hour of the day that you spent filling your belly and gassing about your status q—oh, wasn't I crying "Republic, Republic, Republic?"

So one day, me laddo, you woke up and found that the Republic did live after all. And would you like know why?

Just because I and my like had said so, and said so again, while you were too drunk and too lazy and too thick in the head to say anything at all. That's why. And then, with the rest of your kidney you hunched your shoulders, spat on your hands, and went back to your bed mumbling, "Up the Status q—oh." So why the hell should I try to convince you?

I tell you, we can make this country — this world — whatever we want it to be by saying so, and saying so again. I tell you, it is the knowledge of this that is the genius and glory of the Gael!

THE SCYTHE AND THE SUNSET
by Denis Johnston

Tetley is in his thirties, quiet, and a Commandant in the Irish Volunteers. It is the afternoon of Easter Monday, 1916, and the rebellion is now showing serious signs of collapse.

TETLEY: I don't know what to think. I'd fight to the last building and the last man if I was sure of only one thing — that I was fighting for my country and for my people, and not just for my own satisfaction.

[Emer: Do you doubt that?]

TETLEY: [I'm afraid I do.] Look at that girl over there. You know how she feels about us. Are we fighting for her?

[Roisin: Ye are not.]

[Emer: Who would mind her? She's only a West Briton — a shoneen.]

[Roisin: Call me that again an I'll gut yet for garters. I'm for John Redmond an there's no yella streak in our flag.]

TETLEY: You see. She's the people. It's their hostility that's really shaken me — not any question of whether we're going to win or lose. I was watching their faces during the reading of the proclamation, and there was nothing but derision in those eyes — derision, and that murderous Irish laughter. It was as if we were putting on a rather poor entertainment for them, and they wanted their money back.

[Emer: They'll change. We'll show them.]

TETLEY: [Show them what? That they're downtrodden? You can't show people that if they don't feel it.] There we were — in our hands, the first declaration of our independence for the past seven hundred years. But there was no sign of understanding in those eyes. And then... at the words "Ireland through us summons her children to the flag and strikes for her freedom"...that crash of glass, and that terrible shout of "Noblett's toffee shop." *(He sinks into his chair and covers his face with his hands.)*

Oh, these moments of doubt and self-examination! I can stand anything but them. Do I have to pretend to myself that I'm another Jesus Christ — that everyone's wrong except me? Endymion thinks like that. But I'm a sane man — amn't I?

THE FIELD
by John B. Keane

*The voice of the Bishop interrupts the action of this play concerning a
land dispute in a small Irish village. Visiting from England, William
Dee was attacked and accidentally killed by Bull and Tadhg McCabe,
two local farmers, after bidding against them for a piece of land at a
public auction. Convinced of their own right to the property and re-
sentful of the outsider's bid, they were attempting to intimidate him to
forget about buying the land for his sick wife.*

BISHOP:
"Do not be afraid of those who kill the body but cannot kill the soul.
But rather be afraid of him who is able to destroy both body and soul
in Hell."

In the name of the Father and of the Son and of the Holy Ghost,
Amen.

Dearly beloved brethren, these are the words of Christ himself. He
was speaking about truth. How many of you would deny Christ? How
many of you, like Peter, would stand up and say: "I know not the
Man!" but you can lie without saying a word; you can lie without
opening your lips; you can lie by silence.

Five weeks ago in this parish, a man was murdered — he was bru-
tally beaten to death. For five weeks the police have investigated and
not one single person has come forward to assist them. Everywhere
they turned, they were met by silence, a silence of the most frightful
and diabolical kind — the silence of the lie. In God's name, I beg you,
I implore you, if any of you knows anything, to come forward and
speak without fear.

This is a parish in which you understand hunger. But there are
many hungers. There is a hunger for food — a natural hunger. There
is the hunger of the flesh — a natural understandable hunger. There is
a hunger for home, for love, for children. These things are good —
they are good because they are necessary. But there is also the hunger
for land. And in this parish, you, and your fathers before you knew
what it was to starve because you did not own your own land — and
that has increased; this unappeasable hunger for land. But how far are
you prepared to go to satisfy this hunger. Are you prepared to go to
the point of robbery? Are you prepared to go to the point of murder?

Are you prepared to kill for land? Was this man killed for land? Did he give his life's blood for a field? If so, that field will be a field of blood and it will be paid for in thirty pieces of silver — the price of Christ's betrayal — and you, by your silence will share in that betrayal.

Among you there is a murderer! You may even know his name, you may even have seen him commit this terrible crime — through your silence, you share his guilt, your innocent children will grow up under the shadow of this terrible crime, and you will carry this guilt with you until you face your Maker at the moment of judgment.

If you are afraid to go to the police, then come to your priests, or come to me. And if there is one man among you — one man made after Christ's likeness — he will stand up and say: "There! There he is! There is the murderer!" And that man will have acknowledged Christ before men and Christ will acknowledge him before His Father in Heaven. But if you, by your silence, deny Christ before men, He will disown you in Heaven, and I, as His representative, will have a solemn duty to perform. I will place this parish under interdict and then there will be a silence more terrible than the first. The church bell will be silent: the mass bell will not be heard; the voice of the confessional will be stilled and in your last moment will be the most dreadful silence of all for you will go to face your Maker without the last sacrament on your lips...and all because of your silence now. On God's name, I beg of you to speak before it is too late. "I am the way," says Christ, "and the truth. Do not be afraid of those who can kill the body but cannot kill the soul. But rather, be afraid of him who can destroy both the body and soul in hell."

In the name of the Father and of the Son and of the Holy Ghost, Amen.

THE DEATH AND RESURRECTION OF MR. ROCHE
by Thomas Kilroy

*Kelly and Seamus, both middle-class men in their mid-thirties, have
played a bit too rough with a drinking buddy, and he has been
pushed into the cellar where he has died. Kelly phones his lawyer.*

KELLY:
What d'you think about the telephone call?

The telephone call to me solicitor. Begod, I like that. Oh, I like
that. You can sit contented on yer arse. It's I have to sweat to get us
outta this predicament. When there's trouble you can depend on no
effin' body but yourself and that's a surety. I only have to know. That's
all. I only have to know how I stand. *(Dials the phone.)*

Hello. Oh, hello. Hello, Missus. And how's yerself? Is himself there
at all. I didn't suggest he'd be anywhere else at four o'clock in the
morning. I know he's at home in bed. *(Pause.)* I'm here, in me own
place. No, honest to God, I'm as sober as a bloody judge. Listen,
Missus, it's an emergency. Well, I don't think I ought to say, understand
me. Ah, God, Missus, no. Amn't I telling you it's a bloody emergency.
Listen, listen — here's this much for you — and it's the gospel truth —
the guards are liable to walk in the door any minnit. Isn't that enough
for you to go on with? Now! *(Pause; to SEAMUS.)* Oh, she's the melted
whore that wan. Oh, Jasus, you should have heard the carry-on of her!
Lord Almighty! Would you please, says she, would you please indicate
the nature of your business. And the head hanging off me on this end!
Women! Bloody women! Hello, oh hello. Ah, ah, and how's yourself?
It's Kelly. Kelly. KELLY. Don't you remember me? Sure I was only in
with you a week ago about the traffic accident out in Dolphins' Barn.
No, no, no. I'm not in a traffic accident. It's — it's — it's something
else altogether. Listen, listen, you said to me wan night below Murray's
pub. Kelly, says you, Kelly boy, if you're ever up the spout, if you're
in hot water, day or night — that's what you said — night or day, just
lift the phone. I know we're not in Murray's pub now. I only said that
because that's what you said when we were having a few jars together,
you know. God, I'm not a bloody infant altogether! Well, you see, it's
kinda hard to explain, if you get me. You see a crowd of the lads were

here with me. Here. In me flat. Anyway. Well there was this other fel-low here as well. And he — he — he died. Died! He was — killed. No, no, no, no. No one hit him at all. Oh, it's no nightmare. You can take it from me it's no nightmare. How? Well — he just — well, you see what happened was — he just — well, he just fell down — the holy-hole. Holy-hole! Holy-hole! H-o-l-y — Well, it's a class of a cellar I have here in the flat and thas what I call it, holy-hole. Anyway, when we got him up out of it finally the Doc pronounced him dead.

No, we don't have any doctor here. Let me explain. He's only a class of a medical student, if you get me, but that's what we call him, the Doc. It's a class of a nickname. Right. Well, anyway, yer man has had it. But, what am I going to do? I mean, listen, I'm only anxious to know how I stand. That's all. I only want to know how I stand. Good night. *(Long pause, then slowly puts down the phone.)*

He said he couldn't cope with a story like that at four in the morn-ing. Solicitors! Bloody robbers. He said one thing, though. He said we wouldn't get out of this in a hurry. Godalmighty what came over us to shove him around?

THE BENDING OF THE BOUGH
by George Moore

*Jasper Dean is a dynamic, young alderman in a village in western
Ireland around the turn of the century. He finds himself embroiled in
a conflict between Irish nationalism and loyalty to the British Empire
when he comes under the influence of Ralph Kirwan, a mystic who
dreams of a culturally independent society for Ireland.*

DEAN:

Kirwan, I want to open my heart to you, so that you, who are wise,
may tell me what I really am.

Faith is what I need; outside of faith no life exists; unbelief is an
empty gulf. I have discovered that. And it is that I may get faith that I
seek you so constantly; it is for this that I watch and that I listen; and
the desire of faith in me is so great that my very pores open like thirst-
ing flowers when you speak. It is faith that ennobles and those who
have not faith are conscious of their baseness and of the baseness of
life. When I am with you, Kirwan, all seems true, holy, and worthy;
but when you leave me to myself, when I live among worldlings, the
beliefs you have inspired within me die like leaves, and flutter away.

Some day I shall believe as implicitly as you do in the great unity
of things; I wish to feel when I look at the stars shining or the flowers
growing that all is a great, harmonious song, singing through space
and through the ages; and that each race has its destiny; and that as
no race has looked so long and so steadfastly through the shells of
things out into the beyond as our race, it will be the first to attain this
supreme end; we know the end is union with something beyond,
though words may not further define it; we feel it throbbing always
like a pulse within us.

I am nothing, but I must believe in the sacredness of the land
under foot; I must see in it the birthplace of noble thought, heroism
and beauty, and divine ecstasies. These are souls, and in a far truer
sense than we are souls; this land is the birthplace of our anterior
selves; at once ourselves and our gods. Our gods have not perished;
they have but retired to the lonely hills. And since I've known you,
Kirwan, I've seen them there at evening; they sit there brooding over
our misfortunes, waiting for us to become united with them and with
each other once more. You taught me to understand these things, and

I think that I do not misinterpret your teaching.

All is alive; nothing is dead. Through the trees and clouds we see the eternal face shining as though a veil, and all the air is filled with phantom forms. We are not alone in the world; life is beautiful and eternal if we have faith. Skepticism reveals only baseness. Faith reveals beauty and design. But, Kirwan, I should have met you earlier. The truths which you have spoken have not fallen on barren soil; but they have not taken root yet, and I fear every moment lest the wind should come and blow them away.

THE GUERNICA HOTEL
by Jim Nolan

Joseph Shannon, middle-aged, returns home in the 1990s to his fam-
ily's seaside hotel after eighteen years' absence. His father, Francis, a
faded revolutionary who now feels useless, has sold the hotel and
wishes to retire. Joseph warns his father that he "must not despair."

JOSEPH:

Sounding the echo, remember? Isn't that what you used to say. I was
nine years old and we were coming back from some meeting you
spoke at in a hall in Kilmore. There were half a dozen people in the
hall. Afterwards we cycle home on that great black bike you called the
Chariot. I was on the bar, but you must have been getting old, because
we had to walk up Strand Hill. Then I began to cry and when you
asked me why I said it was because so few people had come to hear
you speak. That was when you said that sounding an echo was the
important thing. You pointed over the cliff to the water below and said
as long as the tide came in and out at Seafield, you'd sound that echo
— even if no-one heard. Then I looked up into your eyes and I saw
that you were crying too. You knew what it would come to didn't you
— no-one listening, nothing changed. Your voice carrying out to a
silent sea. Well, so be it, Francey. But you may keep sounding that
echo. You made those men a promise and you made me one too.

Your son speaks. The child at the waters edge. You gave me something to believe in. It wasn't a political system. It was you. Nothing
could destroy the knowledge that my father was a good man. Love
wasn't just a word, justice an idea, dignity some pious aspiration for
the poor. Those words meant something, didn't they Francis? You
made me believe that. And then one day I looked at you and it was
all gone. *(Pause)*. I've been down a bad road Francis. I spent years
burying in alcohol the memory of you. I tried to kill you by killing myself. When occasionally I surfaced I'd look around me and what I saw
convinced me you were right. It was all just a sordid mess and it would
never change. So I'd go down again, hating you even more for ever
having dared to hope it could be different. But your ghost wouldn't go
away. Everywhere I'd run you'd be there waiting, standing in the
moonlight over Strand Hill, pointing down to the sea below and telling

me that as long as the tide came in and out you'd sound that echo. *(Pause.)* I've stopped running Francis. I haven't come home to save you but to be saved from what I see.

THE GUERNICA HOTEL
by Jim Nolan

At a seaside hotel, a group of faded revolutionaries gathers every year in remembrance of a fallen comrade-in-arms. All are dead now, except for Francis Shannon, who holds his own lonely celebration.

SHANNON:

It was a lie Amelia — I lied! It must be thirty years since we first sat in that room but for half that time and more I've been dancing on Bradford's grave.

He was an Orangeman — can you believe that? A dyed in the wool Proddy from the Shankill Road, as faithful once to that blinkered, stunted vision as I once was to its green equivalent. One June morning, Nineteen hundred and thirty-four, eight of us, IRA to the man cycled sixty miles to the Tone Commemoration at Bodenstown. That same morning, Bradford and his comrades set out from Belfast under the banner of the Shankill Road branch of Republican Congress. Green and Orange marched together under the summer sun. All the old certainties passed away. And d'you know what happened? We stoned them. Not me but mine. Stoned them! Stoned the audacity of the Prods daring to cross the divide and match with us on our sacred ground. The republic lived and died that day, Amelia. You can't wipe out eight hundred years in an afternoon I suppose. Three years later in Spain, he lay dying in my arms and as his life's blood seeped into the Spanish earth, with it seemed to flow the last vestiges of hope. Not that I understood all this at the time. For years afterwards I still believed in miracles. But evil does prevail, hope does fade. And the question I came round to asking was what drunken remembrance would ever restore that belief. Which battle recounted, what verse of the internazionale sung for the umpteenth time would ever achieve anything to make real the dream that Bradford and all the others died for. I'd stopped believing! But I didn't have the courage to tell my comrades. So I lied for eighteen years. And now they've gone. I don't have a reason to lie anymore.

MOONSHINE
by Jim Nolan

McKeever, a middle-aged mortician, was once in love with the town preacher's daughter, Elizabeth. Now Elizabeth's mother has passed away and McKeever is called upon to prepare the body for burial.

MCKEEVER:

(Singing happily on entrance.)
E'er since by faith I saw the stream,
Thy flowing wounds supply
Redeeming love has been my theme
And shall be till I die.

Enfin, le visage! Hands and face, the most important. Visible signs, d'y'see. So. No cock-ups in that department. And there won't be either — not tonight, Josephine! The embalmer, Margaret, is a creator of illusions. We banish the traces of suffering and death and present the deceased in an attitude of normal and restful sleep. We create, as Strub and Frederick so movingly put it, "a memory picture." Good old Strub and Frederick, the unsung heroes of the mortuary. Perhaps you've heard of them, Margaret. Their book, "The Principles and Practice of Embalming" is the veritable bible of our profession. Not exactly coffee table stuff, I grant you, and I don't expect they'll surface in the best-seller lists, but old Strub and Frederick have filled many a lonely hour for me, I can tell you. *(Pause.)* There now, clean as a new pin. (Foreceps and cotton wool.) Next we have the packing of the orifices. Don't worry Margaret, you won't feel a thing. *(Pause.)* You don't mind if I call you Margaret, do you, Margaret? I feel it brings us closer. And after all, I was almost one of the family one time, wasn't I? Of course, you couldn't have known that and I don't suppose it matters to you now but I was yes, very much so.

(Pause. Takes remote control switch from pocket and turns off music.)

We were lovers, y'see. Lizzie and me. That shocked you, didn't it — if you were alive today you'd die of the fright. Yes, lovers. In this very room, too. On this very trolley. Life and death. Would have told you sooner only I didn't think you'd understand. That's why she went away. Nothing to do with you or John, Margaret — it was all McKeever's fault. *(Pause.)* Don't be angry, Margaret — I meant no harm. Please. Don't get upset. It was all right. *(Pause.)* It was all right, that is, until I blew it. I couldn't cut it, Margaret. And the track record, not great. Ask the absent Mrs. McKeever if you don't believe me. Didn't want to repeat history, did we? So I rewrote it instead.

Our father who art in exile, that was me. Never around when he's wanted. *(Sings.)*

I see the moon, the moon sees me
Under the shade of the old oak tree
Please let the moon that shines on me
Shine on the one I love.

BELFRY
by Billy Roche

Artie O'Leary, a sexton in a small Irish town, has had an affair with Angela, his best friend's wife. Now the affair has ended in scandal and shame and Angela has returned to her husband.

ARTIE:

(To the audience.) I know what they think of me. I know well enough what they say about me behind my back. There he goes, Artie O'Leary the poor little sacristan with the candle grease on his sleeve, smellin' of incense as he opens the big heavy belfry door. They watch me standin' quietly in the shadows of the mortuary when they come to bury their dead and they see me goin' home to my little empty house in the rain every night to listen to the news. Lonely auld days and nights they're thinkin'; Dreary auld mornings too. Snuffin' out candles and emptyin' poor boxes. Of course they've all probably forgotten by now that I once loved a woman. Another man's wife. She came into this queer auld whisperin' world of mine to change the flowers in the chapel and to look after the altar and although she's been gone out of here over a year now I swear to God her fragrance still lingers about the place — in the transept, near the shrine. Around the vestry and above in the belfry — her scent...wherever I go...It's thanks to her that I have a past worth talkin' about at all I suppose. Although I often curse her for it. There are days now when I find myself draggin' her memory behind me everywhere I go. I bless her too though. She tapped a hidden reservoir inside of me that I didn't even know was there.

Because of her I now find myself ramblin' into snooker halls and back room card games where, surrounded by archin' eyebrows, I become my father's son again and argue the toss with anyone who cares to step on my corns. And I must confess that I get a certain manly satisfaction from the fact that I can hold my own with the so-called big drinkers and small-time gamblers of the town. Oh yes, a hidden reservoir she tapped...But before we all get carried away here I think I'd better point out to yeh that I'm more a man in mournin' than a hawk in the night. Because yeh see I know now for sure that she will not be comin' back to me. And so I mourn. And I pine. And everytime I come up here the sound of this lonely bell tells me that I'm goin' to live a long, long time. The only consolation I have is that at least now I have a story to tell.

BELFRY
by Billy Roche

*Artie, a small-town sexton in his twenties, has taken under his wing a
mentally handicapped boy, Dominic. He employed him as a custodian for the church until Dominic was sent to an institution.
Concurrently, Artie's mother has passed away after a long, wasting
disease.*

ARTIE:

(To the audience.) Me mother never got over the operation. She lin-
gered in hospital for a few days and then one night she just passed
away peacefully in her sleep. We buried her on a cold dismal day. It
was a small funeral. The next couple of weeks were terrible for me. I
felt as if there was a big black cloud hangin' over me, bearin' down
on me all the time. I'd go back to my little empty house and everywhere I'd turn I'd find somethin' to remind me of her. I felt so lonely,
I swear I'd just want to curl up and die. Then one day I caught a
glimpse of Angela goin' down the street in front of me and all of a sudden the whole thing just sort of lifted. All of a sudden I was my father's son again. I slipped into a bettin' shop to get away from the rain
and while I was waitin' I put a couple of quid on a horse called Baby
Blue. It came in at eight to one. So I went home and I got all dressed
up and that night I went out on the town. I went into a lounge bar to
hear the Ferryman. I had a right night. Later on I rambled into a late
night snooker hall and the whole place turned to look at me. After a
few months though they'd be steppin' back out of my way. I'm not
coddin' yeh the snooker cue just seemed to belong in my hand. A pack
of cards the very same. I've always been blessed with a good memory
and I'm goin' to tell yeh one thing but it didn't take me too long to
fleece a couple of fellas who would have considered themselves
sharks. One fella — Shepherd Kelly — was a bad loser and he reared
up on me one night. I've since discovered of course that all good play-
ers are bad losers, includin' me. Anyway this fella tossed the deck of
cards into my face and called me a jamie bastard and I surprised everyone when I stretched him across the table with a box in the jaw. Oh
yes, a hidden reservoir she tapped...I bought a tombstone for my
mother's grave and a load of those sparkly stones. It looks nice now.
I go out there every Sunday to say a few prayers for her. I hope I won't

have a small funeral. It's nice over there on the other side of the river though. You can taste the tang of the sea and the seaweed and that and all the other little wild things that can't be caught or what-do-you-call-it...tamed. It's kind of wild over there like yeh know...It's nice though!

WHAT IS AN IRISHMAN?
by George Bernard Shaw

This selection is from Preface for Politicians *(1907), which Shaw
added to his earlier work,* John Bull's Other Island, *a commercial success in England. These essays were intended to give Broadbent, the
play's English character, as well as the English audience, a "piece of
[Shaw's] mind, as an Irishman."*

SPEAKER:

When I say that I am an Irishman I mean that I was born in Ireland,
and that my native language is the English of Swift and not the un-
speakable jargon of the midnineteenth century London newspapers.
My extraction is the extraction of most Englishmen: that is, I have no
trace in me of the commercially imported North Spanish strain which
passes for aboriginal Irish: I am a genuine typical Irishman of the
Danish, Norman, Cromwellian, and (of course) Scotch invasions. I am
violently and arrogantly Protestant by family tradition; but let no
English government therefore count on my allegiance: I am English
enough to be an inveterate Republican and Home Ruler. It is true that
one of my grandfathers was an Orangeman; but then his sister was an
abbess and his uncle, I am proud to say, was hanged as a rebel. When
I look round me on the hybrid cosmopolitans, slum poisoned or
square pampered, who call themselves Englishmen today, and see
them bullied by the Irish Protestant garrison as no Bengalee now lets
himself be bullied by an Englishman; when I see the Irishman everywhere standing clear headed, sane, hardily callous to the boyish sen-
timentalities, susceptibilities, and credulities that make the Englishman
the dupe of every charlatan and the idolater of every numskull, I per-
ceive that Ireland is the only spot on earth which still produces the
ideal Englishman of history. Blackguard, bully, drunkard, liar, foul-
mouth, flatterer, beggar, backbiter, venal functionary, corrupt judge,
envious friend, vindictive opponent, unparalleled political traitor: All
these your Irishman may easily be, just as he may be a gentleman (a
species extinct in England, and nobody a penny the worse); but he is
never quite the hysterical, nonsense-crammed, fact-proof, truth-terri-
fied, unballasted sport of all the bogey panics and all the silly enthu-

siasms that now calls itself "God's Englishman." England cannot do without its Irish and its Scots today, because it cannot do without at least a little sanity.

THE SHADOWY WATERS
by William Butler Yeats

Forgael, the captain of a ship in isolated waters, has just awakened.
His crew, however, afraid that he had lost his mind, was plotting a
mutiny while he slept. Fortunately, they have spotted their first ship in
over a month, a spice vessel which they can plunder.

FORGAEL:

(*Who has remained at the tiller.*) There! There! They come!
   Gull, gannet, or diver,
But with a man's head, or a fair woman's.
They hover over the masthead awhile
To wait their friends, but when their friends have come
They'll fly upon that secret way of theirs,
One — and one — a couple — five together.
And now they all wheel suddenly and fly
To the other side, and higher in the air,
They've gone up thither, friend's run up by friend;
They've gone to their beloved ones in the air,
In the waste of the high air, that they may wander
Among the windy meadows of the dawn.
But why are they still waiting? Why are they
Circling and circling over the masthead?
Ah! now they all look down — they'll speak of me
What the Ever-living put into their minds,
And of that shadowless unearthly woman
At the world's end. I hear the message now,
But it's all mystery. There's one that cries,
"From love and hate." Before the sentence ends
Another breaks upon it with a cry,
"From love and death and out of sleep and waking."
And with the cry another cry is mixed,
"What can we do, being shadows?" All mystery,
And I am drunken with a dizzy light.
But why do they still hover overhead?
Why are you circling there? Why do you linger?

Why do you not run to your desire,
Now that you have happy winged bodies?
Being too busy in the air, and the high air,
They cannot hear my voice. But why that circling?
(The sailors have returned. Dectora is with them.)
(Turning and seeing her.) Why are you standing with your eyes
upon me?
You are not the world's core. O no, no, no!
That cannot be the meaning of the birds.
You are not its core.

THE UNICORN FROM THE STARS
by William Butler Yeats

The play takes place in Dublin in the early 19th century. Martin, a young laborer whose religious fervor concerns his family, explains his beliefs to his parish priest.

MARTIN:
Father John, Heaven is not what we have believed it to be. It is not quiet, it is not singing and making music, and all strife at an end. I have seen it, I have been there. The lover still loves, but with a greater passion, and the rider still rides, but the horse goes like the wind and leaps the ridges, and the battle goes on always, always. That is the joy of Heaven, continual battle. I thought the battle was here, and that the joy was to be found here on earth, that all one had to do was bring again the old wild earth of the stories — but no, it is not here; we shall not come to that joy, that battle, till we have put out the senses, everything that can be seen and handled, as I put out this candle. *(He puts out the candle.)* We must put out the whole world as I put out this candle. *(Puts out another candle.)* We must put out the light of the stars and the light of the sun and the light of the moon *(Puts out the rest of the candles.)*, till we have brought everything to nothing once again. I saw in a broken vision, but now all is clear to me. Where there is nothing, where there is nothing — there is God!

NINE SCENES FOR
ONE WOMAN AND ONE MAN

AFTER EASTER
by Anne Devlin

GRETA
CAMPBELL

*Greta, an Irishwoman living in England, sat herself in front of a bus,
hoping that it would run her over. She now finds herself in a mental
hospital arguing with Campbell, an Edinburgh-born psychiatrist.*

GRETA: I have often found when you can't do anything else you can
always sit on the road. It's better than screaming. It makes everyone else scream. It makes me very quiet. My mother used to
scream. She'd run upstairs after me and pull my hair. I'd sit behind
the bedroom door for hours — with the bed pushed up against it.
And she'd scream and scream and pound the door. But she could-
n't get in. Nobody could. After a while she'd stop and go downstairs. And she'd forget about it. Then I'd put my head down and
go to sleep. She'd shout, "Nobody loves you! Nobody loves you!"
And I'd think it doesn't matter because I love me. I don't need anyone. And then I'd tickle myself, and that would make me smile.
Until one day — there was a day we collected outside the university, it was a small march from the Students' Union. And just at the
beginning as we linked up to start — I was in the front row, it was
very peaceful — we linked arms and suddenly I had this rush of
things, as if everything was suddenly centered in one place and it
started to move, and it started to make me smile, and I kept trying not to smile; but the smile kept coming until I couldn't hold it
back any longer and it grew and grew so big. And then we
stepped forward and moved off.

I didn't go on any more marches after that. The rest of the day
seemed very flat, it seemed to me — as if that was the point. And
anyway lots of other things make me smile...the sun shining
through the bedroom window on my cunt.
*(The lights in the room brighten. It is a hospital room somewhere
in England. The man who is a doctor moves in on Greta.)*
CAMPBELL: Do you still think you're the Virgin Mary?
GRETA: Och, I think everyone is the Virgin Mary. *(He shakes his head
gravely at this.)*

CAMPBELL: When asked why you refused to return to your house, you said, "It's a Protestant house."

GRETA: Well it's true. It feels very Presbyterian, that house. I have tried. I stripped the door and sanded the floors and painted all the walls green and white — but I look at it and it's defeated me, I find I can't change it. It is a Protestant house.

CAMPBELL: When asked about your relationship with your mother, you said, "Venus is my mother."

GRETA: It's a line from a poem.

CAMPBELL: What poem is that?

GRETA: I haven't written it yet.

CAMPBELL: That is the kind of response that's keeping you here, Greta!

GRETA: Is it my fault if people are so literal?

CAMPBELL: When the nurse brought in your baby, you said: "This is not my baby."

GRETA: I was expressing my grief.

CAMPBELL: I'm afraid the committee took it as evidence that you were still rejecting the child.

GRETA: My baby was taken away from me at two-and-a-half weeks. When they brought it back later it wasn't my baby any more. I was grieving over the days I'd stopped breast-feeding him. He'd grown up and I knew I could never get that time back. They put him on powdered milk and it blew him up, he was fat. That was why I said, "This is not my baby." I'd lost that baby.

CAMPBELL: I am trying to help you.

GRETA: I want to go home.

CAMPBELL: To your husband?

GRETA: To my mother.

CAMPBELL: I understand that you don't get on with your mother. Why?

GRETA: Why what?

CAMPBELL: Why do you want to go home to your mother?

GRETA: I want to make my father jealous. I want to seduce my mother — in fact, I want to seduce you.

CAMPBELL: *(He is about to leave the room.)* Goodbye Greta.

GRETA: I don't know which is worse — your moral good health or your hypocrisy!

CAMPBELL: My hypocrisy?

GRETA: Most men want to sleep with every attractive woman they meet. And that is normal. I want to sleep with most men — and that is not normal. And I'm not supposed to say it. Isn't that the point? I'm not — supposed — to — use — the — words!

CAMPBELL: Why won't you return to your husband?

GRETA: My husband doesn't want me.

CAMPBELL: Is that why you threw yourself in front of a bus?

GRETA: But I didn't.

CAMPBELL: You did, Greta. We have to agree about this piece of reality. A bus is a very substantial thing — it is not in your head, it is out there on the road. And this is your body, and it is real and substantial and if you put your body in front a moving bus it will kill you. Now I have to find out if it was your intention or not. If it was your intention, you are staying here.

GRETA: And if it wasn't my intention?

CAMPBELL: You may be even more dangerous.

GRETA: So either way, I'm staying here?

CAMPBELL: Not necessarily.

GRETA: Look, if I sat down on the road with twenty people I'd have been arrested. Because I sat down on the road on my own it was a suicide attempt. Confirms what I've always suspected — the difference between insanity and politics is only a matter of numbers!

CAMPBELL: So you weren't trying to kill yourself — it was a political act? Why? What were you protesting about?

GRETA: *(Inaudibly.)* Boredom.

CAMPBELL: (He hasn't heard properly.) I'm sorry?

GRETA: I was bored. I ran out of a room where some people were having dinner and I sat down on the road...I may even have resented that one of the people — the woman giving the dinner party — had flown with the asparagus from Italy that morning. I may have been jealous that she was a rich art critic, that everyone at the table was a critic of one kind or another. And I had so far failed to be even a poor artist. I may even have minded that the art critic was my husband's mistress. I said something harsh and made some Englishman's wife cry.

CAMPBELL: Why do you resent being Irish so much?

GRETA: I don't resent being Irish — I only resent it being pointed out to me. I suppose I am beginning to resent being the only Irish person at every gathering.

CAMPBELL: Why don't you meet with some other Irish people?

GRETA: I don't know any, I live in Oxford...Anyway it seems a bit vulgar, you know to go out looking for people who have the same or a similar accent. Oh I know it's something you English do all the time, but frankly that's a good reason for not doing it.

CAMPBELL: Why is this such a big thing with you people? I come from Scotland, but it's not important to me.

GRETA: *(She studies him.)* Och, you're a cod!

CAMPBELL: I understand you want a divorce.

GRETA: My husband says I talk too much.

CAMPBELL: You won't get custody of the children.

GRETA: What?

CAMPBELL: Do you think in your present circumstances that any court would let you have care of the children?

GRETA: Oh God! then there isn't any point.

CAMPBELL: I am thinking of letting you out for Easter to stay with your sister.

GRETA: That's impossible! My sister lives in Toome.

CAMPBELL: Where?

GRETA: Toomebridge. Northern Ireland. I don't think she'd have me.

CAMPBELL: You have two sisters.

GRETA: Ah well, my other sister is a highly successful something or other. She's not in touch with the family — I haven't seen her for years.

CAMPBELL: Do you want out of here?

GRETA: Of course I want out of here.

(He goes to the door.)

GRETA: Dr. Campbell? Wait! Please!

(He exits.)

GRETA: *(Muttering.)* I never thought I was the Virgin Mary anyway. I just hope to Christ I'm not John the Baptist. *(Begins to sing.)*

My bonny lies over the ocean.
My bonny lies over the sea.
My bonny lies over the ocean.
Oh bring back my bonny to me.

(In a different voice.) Stop that singing!

(Begins again, falteringly.) Bring back, oh bring back, Oh bring back my bonny to me, to me — *(Stops dead.)*

LOVERS
by Brian Friel

JOE
MAG

On a spring day, Mag and Joe, both seventeen, ascend a hill which overlooks their village. They had been intent on studying for final exams, but the conversation quickly turns to their new flat. They hope to move in after their upcoming marriage, made necessary due to Mag's pregnancy.

JOE: I signed the lease yesterday evening.

MAG: *(Absolutely thrilled.)* It's ours now? We own it?

JOE: Old Kerrigan was so busy working he wouldn't take time off to go into the office; so we put the document on the back of a cow that was about to be shot and that's where we signed it. Cockeyed old miser!

MAG: He's not!

JOE: What?

MAG: Cockeyed.

JOE: I'm telling you. And crazy, too. In a big rubber apron and him dripping with blood. And cows and sheep and bullocks dropping dead all around him.

MAG: Oh God, my stomach!

(JOE realizes that his tale is successful. He gets up on his feet to enact the scene. MAG listens with delight and soon gets drawn into the pantomime.)

JOE: "Drive him up there! Another beast. C'mon! C'mon! I haven't all day. And what's bothering you, young Brennan? Steady, there. Steady! Bang! Bang! Drag it away! Slit its throat! Slice it open! Skin it!"

MAG: Stop-stop!

JOE: Another beast! Get a move on! What am I paying you fellas for? You told me about the flat, Mr. Kerrigan. "Steady—bang! Bang! Damnit, I nearly missed—bang!—that's it. Drag him off. What are you saying, young Brennan? The lease? Oh, the lease! Oh, aye. Here we are." *(JOE produces an imaginary document from his hip pocket.)* "Best flat in town. Hell, it's all blood now." *(JOE wipes the imaginary document on his leg.)* "Come on! Another animal!

There's a fine beast for you, young Brennan! Look at those shanks! Bang! Bang! Never knew what hit him! I sign here, son, don't I?" *(JOE pretends to write: but the pen does not work and he flings it away.)* "Hell, that doesn't write."

MAG: Bang! Bang!

JOE: "Keep behind me, young Brennan. This is a dangerous job."

MAG: Let's sign it in blood, young Brennan.

JOE: "Finest view in town. And the noise down here's great company. Bang! Bang!

MAG: Like living in Dead Man's Creek.

JOE: There's a bullock that looks like the president of Saint Kevin's. Bang! Bang!

MAG: A sheep the image of Sister Paul. Bang! Bang!

JOE: Drag 'em away!

MAG: Slice 'em open!

JOE: Joan O'Hara's white poodle, Tweeny.

MAG: Bang! And Philip Moran's mother.

JOE: Bang! Bang! Doctor Watson.

MAG: A friend. Pass, friend, pass.

JOE: Skinny Skeehan, the solicitor.

MAG: Bang-bang-bang-bang! Look — reverend mother!

JOE: Where?

MAG: To the right—behind the rocks!

JOE: *(Calling sweetly.)* Mother Dolores.

MAG: *(Answering sweetly.)* Yes, Joseph?

JOE: *(Viciously)* Bang-bang-bang!

(MAG grabs her stomach and falls slowly.)

MAG: Into thy hands, O Lord —

JOE: Bang!

(The final bullet enters her shoulder.)

MAG: O shite-!

(MAG rolls on the ground, helpless with laughter.)

JOE: The town clerk — bang! All the teachers — bang!

MAG: The church choir —

JOE: Bang! Everyone that lives along snobby, snotty Melville Road — bang-bang-bang-bang-bang!

MAG: A holy-cost, by God.

(JOE listens attentively. Silence.)

JOE: Everything's quiet. Now we'll have peace to study. Back to the books.

MAG: I'm sore all over. (*Searching.*) Give us a fag quick.

JOE: (*Bashfully.*) I'm afraid — I — sort of — sort of lost my head there, ma'am.

MAG: Does your mother know you act the clown like that?

JOE: Does your father know you smoke? Look at the time it is! I came here to work.

(*He goes back to his books. He is immediately immersed.*)

MAG: Joe...

JOE: What?

MAG: The flat's ours now?

JOE: Isn't that what I'm telling you.

MAG: You're sure you wouldn't like the top floor in our house?

JOE: Positive.

MAG: (*After a moment's hesitation.*) So am I. I just wanted to know if you were, too.

JOE: Goodbye.

MAG: It's only that Papa'll be lonely without me. For his sake, really. But he'll get over that. And it's just that this is the first time he'll ever have been separated from me, even for a night. But he'll get over it. All parents have to face it sooner or later. (*Happily.*) Besides, I can wheel the pram over every afternoon. (*She looks at JOE, lost in his books: and again she has the momentary dread of the exam.*) I'm like you, Joe. When I concentrate, you could yell at me and I wouldn't hear you.

(*She opens a book — almost at random. Looks at the sky.*)

It's going to be very warm...

(*She takes off her school blazer, rolls up the sleeves of her blouse, and stretches out under the sun.*)

If we didn't have to work, we could sun bathe.

TRANSLATIONS
by Brian Friel

YOLLAND
MAIRE

Maire, a vibrant Irishwoman of twenty, finds herself and her village changing upon the arrival of English cartographers, who are changing the Gaelic names of places. Yolland is a young English soldier who has been sent to the village to execute this task. The two, having left a dance, attempt to communicate despite the huge language and cultural barriers between them. (Note: Though Friel has used English to convey most of their thoughts, they are actually speaking their own languages, in most places, and don't understand one another.)

MAIRE: Oh my God, that leap across the ditch nearly killed me.

YOLLAND: I could scarcely keep up with you.

MAIRE: Wait till I get my breath back.

YOLLAND: We must have looked as if we were being chased.

(They now realise they are alone and holding hands — the beginnings of embarrassment. The hands drift apart. Pause.)

MAIRE: Manus'll wonder where I've got to.

YOLLAND: I wonder did anyone notice us leave.

(Pause. Slightly further apart.)

MAIRE: The grass must be wet. My feet are soaking.

YOLLAND: Your feet must be wet. The grass is soaking.

(Another pause. Another few paces apart. They are now a long distance from one another.)

YOLLAND: *(Indicating himself.)* George.

(MAIRE nods: Yes-yes. Then:)

MAIRE: Lieutenant George.

YOLLAND: Don't call me that. I never think of myself as Lieutenant.

MAIRE: What-what?

YOLLAND: Sorry-sorry? (*He points to himself again.*) George.

(MAIRE nods: Yes-yes. Then points to herself.)

MAIRE: Maire.

YOLLAND: Yes, I know you're Maire. Of course I know you're Maire. I mean I've been watching you night and day for the past...

MAIRE: *(Eagerly.)* What-what?

YOLLAND: *(Points.)* Maire. *(Points.)* George. *(Points both.)* Maire and
George. (Maire nods: Yes-yes-yes.) I — I — I —
MAIRE: Say anything at all. I love the sound of your speech.
YOLLAND: *(Eagerly.)* Sorry-sorry? *(In acute frustration he looks
around, hoping for some inspiration that will provide him with
communicative means. Now he has a thought: he tries raising his
voice and articulating in a staccato style and with equal and ab-
surd emphasis on each word.)* Every-morning-I-see-you-feeding-
brown-hens-and-giving-meal-to-black-calf — (The futility of it.) —
O my God.
*(MAIRE smiles. She moves towards him. She will try to communi-
cate in Latin.)*
MAIRE: Tue es centturio in — in — in exercitu Britanico —
YOLLAND: Yes-yes? Go on — go on — say anything at all — I love
the sound of your speech.
MAIRE: — et es in castris quae-quae-quae sunt in agro—
— O my God. *(YOLLAND smiles. He moves towards her. Now for
her English words.)* George-water.
YOLLAND: "Water"? Water! Oh yes — water — water — very good —
water — good — good.
MAIRE: Fire.
YOLLAND: Fire — indeed — wonderful — fire, fire, fire — splendid
— splendid!
MAIRE: Ah...ah...
YOLLAND: Yes? Go on.
MAIRE: Earth.
YOLLAND: "Earth"?
MAIRE: Earth. Earth. *(YOLLAND still does not understand. Maire stoops
down and picks up a handful of clay. Holding it out.)* Earth.
YOLLAND: Earth! Of course — earth! Earth. Earth. Good Lord, Maire,
your English is perfect!
MAIRE: *(Eagerly.)* What-what?
YOLLAND: Perfect English. English perfect.
MAIRE: George —
YOLLAND: That's beautiful — oh that's really beautiful.
MAIRE: George —
YOLLAND: Say it again — say it again —
MAIRE: Shhh. *(She holds her hand up for silence — she is trying to re-
member her one line of English. Now she remembers it and she de-*

livers the line as if English were her language — easily, fluidly, con-
versationally.)

George, in Norfolk we besport ourselves around the maypoll.

YOLLAND: Good God, do you? That's where my mother comes from
— Norfolk. Norwich actually. Not exactly Norwich town but a
small village called Little Walsingham close beside it. But in our
own village of Winfarthing we have a maypole too and every year
on the first of May — *(He stops abruptly, only now realising. He
stares at her. She in turn misunderstands his excitement.)*

MAIRE: *(To herself.)* Mother of God, my Aunt Mary wouldn't have
taught me something dirty, would she?
*(Pause. YOLLAND extends his hand to MAIRE. She turns away
from him and moves slowly across the stage.)*

YOLLAND: Maire. *(She still moves away.)* Marie Chatach. *(She still
moves away.)* Bun na hAbhann? *(He says the name softly, almost
privately, very tentatively, as if he were searching for a sound she
might respond to. He tries again.)* Druim Dubh? *(MAIRE stops. She
is listening. YOLLAND is encouraged.)* Poll na gCaorach. Lis Maol.
(MAIRE turns towards him.) Lis na nGall.

MAIRE: Lis na nGradh. *(They are now facing each other and begin
moving — almost imperceptibly — towards each other.)* Carraig an
Phoill.

YOLLAND: Carraig na Ri. Loch nEan.

MAIRE: Loch an Iubhair. Machaire Buidhe.

YOLLAND: Machaire Mor. Cnoc na Mona.

MAIRE: Cnoc na nGabhar.

YOLLAND: Mullach.

MAIRE: Port.

YOLLAND: Tor.

MAIRE: Lag. *(She holds out her hands to YOLLAND. He takes them.
Each now speaks almost to himself/herself.)*

YOLLAND: I wish to God you could understand me.

MAIRE: Soft hands; a gentleman's hands.

YOLLAND: Because if you could understand me I could tell you how
I spend my days either thinking of you or gazing up at your house
in the hope that you'll appear even for a second.

MAIRE: Every evening you walk by yourself along the Tra Bhan and
every morning you wash yourself in front of your tent.

YOLLAND: I would tell you how beautiful you are, curly-headed Maire. I would so like to tell you how beautiful you are.

MAIRE: Your arms are long and thin and the skin on your shoulders is very white.

YOLLAND: I would tell you...

MAIRE: Don't stop — I know what you're saying.

YOLLAND: I would tell you how I want to be here — to live here — always — with you — always, always.

MAIRE: "Always?" What is that word — "always?"

YOLLAND: Yes-yes; always.

MAIRE: You're trembling.

YOLLAND: Yes, I'm trembling because of you.

MAIRE: I'm trembling, too. *(She holds his face in her hand.)*

YOLLAND: I've made up my mind...

MAIRE: Shhhh.

YOLLAND: I'm not going to leave here...

MAIRE: Shhh-listen to me. I want you, too, soldier.

YOLLAND: Don't stop — I know what you're saying.

MAIRE: I want to live with you — anywhere — anywhere at all — always —always.

YOLLAND: "Always"? What is that word — "always"?

MAIRE: Take me away with you, George.

(Pause. Suddenly they kiss.)

EXILES
by James Joyce

ROBERT

BERTHA

> *Bertha agrees to meet Robert, her husband's best friend, at his cabin
> to discuss their future together. However, she has no real intention of
> leaving her husband, as she has told him about Robert's proposals to
> her. Despite this, Robert still loves her.*

ROBERT: *(Touches her shoulder.)* Tell me if the air is too cold for you.
(Half rising.) I will close it.

BERTHA: *(Detaining him.)* No. I am not cold. Besides, I am going
now, Robert. I must.

ROBERT: *(Firmly.)* No, no. There is no must now. We were left here
for this. And you are wrong, Bertha. The past is not past. It is present here now. My feeling for you is the same now as it was then,
because then — you slighted it.

BERTHA: No, Robert. I did not.

ROBERT: *(Continuing.)* You did. And I have felt it all these years without knowing it — till now. Even while I lived — the kind of life
you know and dislike to think of — the kind of life to which you
condemned me.

BERTHA: I?

ROBERT: Yes, when you slighted the common simple gift I had to
offer you — and took his gift instead.

BERTHA: *(Looking at him.)* But you never...

ROBERT: No. Because you had chosen him. I saw that. I saw it on the
first night we met, we three together. Why did you choose him?

BERTHA: *(Bends her head.)* Is that not love?

ROBERT: *(Continuing.)* And every night when we two — he and I —
came to that corner to meet you I saw it and felt it. You remember the corner, Bertha?

BERTHA: *(As before.)* Yes.

ROBERT: And when you and he went away for your walk and I went
along the street alone I felt it. And when he spoke to me about
you and told me he was going away — then most of all.

BERTHA: Why then most of all?

ROBERT: Because it was then that I was guilty of my first treason towards him.

BERTHA: Robert, what are you saying? Your first treason against Dick?

ROBERT: *(Nods.)* And not my last. He spoke of you and himself. Of how your life would be together — free and all that. Free, yes! He would not even ask you to go with him. *(Bitterly.)* He did not. And you went all the same.

BERTHA: I wanted to be with him. You know...*(Raising her head and looking at him.)* You know how we were then — Dick and I.

ROBERT: *(Unbending.)* I advised him to go alone — not to take you with him — to live alone in order to see if what he felt for you was a passing thing which might ruin your happiness and his career.

BERTHA: Well, Robert. It was unkind of you towards me. But I forgive you because you were thinking of his happiness and mine.

ROBERT: *(Bending closer to her.)* No, Bertha. I was not. And that was my treason. I was thinking of myself — that you might turn from him when he had gone and he from you. Then I would have offered you my gift. You know what it was now. The simple common gift that men offer to women. Not the best perhaps. Best or worst — it would have been yours.

BERTHA: *(Turning away from him.)* He did not take your advice.

ROBERT: *(As before.)* No. And the night you ran away together — O, how happy I was!

BERTHA: *(Pressing his hands.)* Keep calm, Robert. I know you liked me always. Why did you not forget me?

ROBERT: *(Smiles bitterly.)* How happy I felt as I came back along the quays and saw in the distance the boat lit up, going down the black river, taking you away from me! (In a calmer tone.) But why did you choose him? Did you not like me at all?

BERTHA: Yes. I liked you because you were his friend. We often spoke about you. Often and often. Every time you wrote or sent papers or books to Dick. And I like you still, Robert. *(Looking into his eyes.)* I never forgot you.

ROBERT: Nor I you. I knew I would see you again. I knew it the night you went away — that you would come back. And that was why I wrote and worked to see you again — here.

BERTHA: And here I am. You were right.

ROBERT: *(Slowly.)* Nine years. Nine times more beautiful!

BERTHA: *(Smiling.)* But am I? What do you see in me?

ROBERT: *(Gazing at her.)* A strange and beautiful lady.

BERTHA: *(Almost disgusted.)* O, please don't call me such a thing!

ROBERT: *(Earnestly.)* You are more. A young and beautiful queen.

BERTHA: *(With a sudden laugh.)* O, Robert!

ROBERT: *(Lowering his voice and bending nearer to her.)* But do you not know that you are a beautiful human being? Do you not know that you have a beautiful body? Beautiful and young?

BERTHA: *(Gravely.)* Some day I will be old.

ROBERT: *(Shakes his head.)* I cannot imagine it. Tonight you are young and beautiful. Tonight you have come back to me. *(With passion.)* Who knows what will be tomorrow? I may never see you again or never see you as I do now.

BERTHA: Would you suffer?

ROBERT: *(Looks around the room, without answering.)* This room and this hour were made for your coming. When you have gone — all is gone.

BERTHA: *(Anxiously.)* But you will see me again, Robert...as before.

ROBERT: *(Looks full at her.)* To make him — Richard — suffer.

BERTHA: He does not suffer.

ROBERT: *(Bowing his head.)* Yes, yes. He does.

BERTHA: He knows we like each other. Is there any harm, then?

ROBERT: *(Raising his head.)* No there is no harm. Why should we not? He does not know yet what I feel. He has left us alone here at night, at this hour, because he longs to know it — he longs to be delivered.

BERTHA: From what?

ROBERT: *(Moves closer to her and presses her arm as he speaks.)* From every law, Bertha, from every bond. All his life he has sought to deliver himself. Every chain but one he has broken and that one we are to break. Bertha — you and I.

BERTHA: *(Almost inaudibly.)* Are you sure?

ROBERT: *(Still more warmly.)* I am sure that no law made by man is sacred before the impulse of passion. *(Almost fiercely.)* Who made us for one only? It is a crime against our own being if we are so. There is no law before impulse. Laws are for slaves. Bertha, say my name! Let me hear your voice say it. Softly!

BERTHA: *(Softly.)* Robert!

ROBERT: *(Puts his arm around her shoulder.)* Only the impulse towards youth and beauty does not die. *(He points towards the porch.)* Listen!

BERTHA: *(In alarm.)* What?

ROBERT: The rain falling. Summer rain on the earth. Night rain. The darkness and warmth and flood of passion. Tonight the earth is loved — loved and possessed. Her lover's arms around her; and she is silent. Speak, dearest!

BERTHA: *(Suddenly leans forward and listens intently.)* Hush!

ROBERT: *(Listening, smiles.)* Nothing. Nobody. We are alone.
(A gust of wind blows in through the porch, with a sound of shaken leaves. The flame of the lamp leaps.)

BERTHA: *(Pointing to the lamp.)* Look!

ROBERT: Only the wind. We have light enough from the other room. *(He stretches his hand across the table and puts out the lamp. The light from the doorway of the bedroom crosses the place where they sit. The room is quite dark.)*

ROBERT: Are you happy? Tell me.

BERTHA: I am going now, Robert. It is very late. Be satisfied.

ROBERT: *(Caressing her hair.)* Not yet, not yet. Tell me, do you love me a little?

BERTHA: I like you, Robert. I think you are good. *(Half rising.)* Are you satisfied?

ROBERT: *(Detaining her, kisses her hair.)* Do not go, Bertha! There is time still. Do you love me too? I have waited a long time. Do you love us both — him and also me? Do you, Bertha? The truth! Tell me. Tell me with your eyes. Or speak!
(She does not answer. In the silence the rain is heard falling.)

THE PATRICK PEARSE MOTEL
by Hugh Leonard

DERMOD
MISS MANNING

> *Dermod, on a business trip away from his wife, finds himself in the path of the hotel's new manageress, Miss Manning. She has been spurned by the man with whom Dermod's wife is having an affair and looks to make up for lost time.*

DERMOD: Miss Manning, you don't have to inspect every room in the building.

MISS MANNING: But I do, it's my job. Besides, my quarters, as charming as they are, really do quite reek of paint...

DERMOD: I'm sorry about that...

MISS MANNING: So we must find me another little nest, hmm? Who is in this room?

DERMOD: Parnell. *(She waits for him to open the door. He does so. She goes in.)*

MISS MANNING: 'nk yow!

DERMOD: The rooms are really all the same.

MISS MANNING: This one isn't. I spy with my little eye something beginning with "n".

DERMOD: "N"?

MISS MANNING: *(Holding up Grainne's nightdress.)* For night attire.

DERMOD: How did that get there?

MISS MANNING: Oh, innocent Amy. As if you didn't know!

DERMOD: I don't.

MISS MANNING: You mean you haven't been entertaining young ladies here on the sly?

DERMOD: Miss Manning, what an idea!

MISS MANNING: Yes, isn't it? *(Examining the nightdress.)* I call this quite saucy.

DERMOD: If that night watchman has been letting couples in here for immoral purposes, I'll kick him the length of the building. That's funny...

MISS MANNING: What is?

DERMOD: I — once bought my wife a nightdress like this.

MISS MANNING: Silly man. Of course she didn't wear it.

DERMOD: How do you know?

MISS MANNING: Wives never do. They can't bear the disappointed look on a man's face when he realizes that underneath the mint sauce is the same old mutton. *(She coughs modestly.)*

DERMOD: *(Stiffly.)* As it happens, Miss Manning, my wife is an attractive woman.

MISS MANNING: Saddle of lamb? How nice.

DERMOD: And the nightdress was accidentally set fire to.

MISS MANNING: You were there?

DERMOD: She showed me the ashes.

MISS MANNING: *(Drily.)* There's no fooling you, is there, Mr. Gibbon?

DERMOD: So if this room is to your liking...

MISS MANNING: I'm not sure. *(Pointing to the portrait.)* Who is he?

DERMOD: Charles Stewart Parnell. My partner didn't want a room named after him, but we ran short of patriots. He destroyed himself because of a woman — an English woman.

MISS MANNING: This room will do nicely.

DERMOD: Good, I'll get your suitcase from reception.

MISS MANNING: It's been such a day. I can't face the thought of unpacking. And all my pretties are at the bottom.

DERMOD: Oh, yes?

MISS MANNING: Of my suitcase, Mr. Gibbon. *(Holding the nightdress.)* I know — why don't I wear this?

DERMOD: That?

MISS MANNING: Finders keepers, losers weepers. And as you can see, I'm the kind of woman who will wear any old thing. Let's hope this one won't go on fire.

DERMOD: Why, do you smoke in bed?

MISS MANNING: I was thinking of spontaneous combustion. Mr. Gibbon, would you be so kind as to fetch me my little vanity case...

DERMOD: Certainly.

MISS MANNING: And then I hope you won't be in a hurry to be off.

DERMOD: Well, I...

MISS MANNING: *(Reclining on the bed.)* Because it's lonelier here than I had imagined. Also, there is such a thing as loneliness of the soul. Did I mention that my gentleman friend has left me?

DERMOD: I'm sorry to hear it.

MISS MANNING: 'nk yow! It happened after the party — the night you and I met. Mr. Gibbon, you see before you a woman scorned. I gave that man the best nights of my life — and of his, too — and he threw me aside like an old bedsock. In my bitterness — *(All in one breath.)* — I even thought of yielding my body to the first man with whom I should happen to find myself alone in a bedroom in a deserted building on a mountainside at dead of night, but of course that would have been silly. *(She looks at him inquiringly.)*

DERMOD: *(His voice trembling.)* Not necessarily.

MISS MANNING: *(Kneeling up on the bed.)* No? Mr. Gibbon, I hope you're not about to make an erotic proposal.

DERMOD: *(Retreating.)* I wasn't.

MISS MANNING: I mean, just because we happen to be alone in a bedroom in a deserted building on a mountainside at dead of night...

DERMOD: Are we?

MISS MANNING: Aren't we?

DERMOD: *(Hoarsely.)* Yes.

MISS MANNING: *(Seizing him.)* So kindly don't come any closer.

DERMOD: I won't.

MISS MANNING: *(Pulling him on to the bed.)* You aren't listening, are you? I mean it — not another step. *(She is now as close to him as she can get. She puts her arms around him, as if on the point of fainting.)* There now. I knew I shouldn't be safe with you. Mr. Gibbon, this is madness. Think what Mrs. Gibbon would say —

DERMOD: I am.

MISS MANNING: — if you were silly enough to tell her. *(Dermod attempts to return her embrace. At once she breaks away. Firmly.)* No, it's too soon. The wounds go too deep. I shall need time.

DERMOD: *(Crestfallen.)* Of course.

MISS MANNING: Five minutes?

DERMOD: I'll get your vanity case. *(Dermod goes out and hurries off up stage towards Reception. Miss Manning heads for the bathroom. On the way she sees the fur coat, which is on the floor where Fintan dropped it and has hitherto been hidden by the bed. She picks it up.)*

MISS MANNING: *(Casually.)* Oh — nice. *(Carrying it into the bathroom.)* James Usheen, I will be revenged on you this night! *(Miss Manning goes off.)*

YOUTH'S THE SEASON
by Mary Manning

TOOTS
DESMOND

Desmond had been working with his sister Deidre in their drawing room until Toots Ellerslie arrived. Toots' penchant for gossip drives Deidre away, while Desmond and Toots continue to exchange news.

TOOTS: That's enough! Poor Deirdre. What is the matter with her anyway? *(She takes off her hat, and examines her face in the glass.)*

DESMOND: Now let's gossip. Let's be vilely libellous. Let's be salacious and treacherous. Let's stab our best friends in the back. Let's betray our relations; let's wash our dirty linen in the drawing room. In other words — let's be Dublin.

TOOTS: Oh do, do, do! I feel like a murder party. *(She sits down facing him.)* Now, is Deirdre going to be married soon? People are beginning to ask when? And why is she so moody?

DESMOND: One question at a time, darling. She's moody because Gerald was two minutes late for an appointment. And she's going to be married when Gerald's in a position to marry —

TOOTS: *(Nodding.)* I see! One of those Five-Year Plans! Well, she's certainly getting poor darling Gerald house-trained in good time. Gerald's rather a lamb, but *he's* full of ruthless medical efficiency too, and he's such a careful young man.

DESMOND: He has to be. All rising young doctors have to be very careful. Very, very careful, dear.

TOOTS: I never could understand why he fell for Deirdre. All Gerald wants is a wee wifie just for breeding and laying out his slippers, but you could hardly describe Deirdre as a wee wifie.

DESMOND: That's where you're wrong, Diana Ellerslie. Deirdre really is a wee wifie, underneath. It's her voluptuous bustle and bust appearance that captivated Gerald. It appealed to his latent Victorianism.

TOOTS: How strange it all is! *(At the window.)* Hallo! There's Philip Pryce arriving back from London. He *is* a dull little boy, isn't he? Why is it that frightfully rich people are invariably frightfully dull? Look at Philip's nice blue overcoat, his bowler hat, his neatly-folded umbrella. I see him every morning going to his father's office just a minute before ten. On Saturday morning he gets a book out of the library, an interesting novel, recommended by the Book Society; and on Saturday afternoon he plays golf; in the evening he joins some nice little party of four — never two; — on Sunday he plays golf. And he drives a very nice little two-seater, and twice a year he goes to London and sees all the best plays, recommended by the best critics; and he has been known to go to the Winter Sports, and once he went to Paris. Soon he'll take unto himself a wife and they'll buy a house with a tennis court at Carrickmines, Foxrock, or Killiney. Two years after they'll have a son and they'll call him Philip Pryce...

DESMOND: *(Jumping up and tearing his hair.)* If you don't stop I'll go mad!

TOOTS: *(Relentlessly.)*...and he'll die and be buried in a well-kept grave, and when the Last Trump sounds, he'll arise with his umbrella neatly folded, and report himself for Judgment just a minute before ten.

DESMOND: And why not? Isn't he normal and clean and healthy — the backbone of the nation? What would we do without Philip Pryce? O God, I'm so depressed!

TOOTS: So am I.

DESMOND: I'm sick of everything, sick of myself, and unutterably sick of Dublin.

TOOTS: It's only a mood. It'll pass.

DESMOND: *(Pacing wildly up and down.)* The umbrella — the symbolic umbrella. That's what I want to escape...Father's office, the bowler hat, and the umbrella. Ah, don't laugh at me!

TOOTS: I'm not laughing. Go on.

DESMOND: I won't give in. I *won't*. Listen Toots — this is serious. You know Derek Howard — well, he wants me to go over to London and take a job there as designer. The pay would be small, at first, but I can persuade Father to give me an allowance for the first year or two, until I get a rise, then everything would be all right. I'm not going to dabble in this duckpond any longer.

TOOTS: You're right! How I envy you! O boy, if only I had your courage.

DESMOND: *(Bitterly.)* Courage! I've no courage. I haven't the guts to get out myself. It all depends on Father, and you know he's set his heart on my going into the office. But he might be made to understand — he might be...

TOOTS: Couldn't your Mother persuade him?

DESMOND: That's my only hope. I'm going to tell her this evening.

TOOTS: Oh Desmond, I do hope she does.

DESMOND: I don't know why I feel so depressed today. I woke up this morning with the most awful feeling of apprehension...

TOOTS: It's the weather. March is always a hideously restless stormy kind of month. Spring in the blood...

DESMOND: It's worse than that. I often have presentiments, and I have one now. Something is going to happen in this house, something evil and overwhelming...

TOOTS: *Don't,* Desmond! My nerves!

DESMOND: *(Going over to the mirror.)* Don't take me seriously, darling. *(He combs his hair carefully.)* What are the wild waves saying? My hair is quite nice I think — don't you, Toots? I'll shoot myself when I go bald. You know I often think it would be amusing if our real selves, the inner man, or still small voice, or whatever it is, would suddenly take human form and confront us.

TOOTS: God forbid. I'd be embarrassed.

DESMOND: We all cover up our real self under a dust-heap of trivialities; but occasionally it insists on being heard.

TOOTS: Well, don't let it get hold of you. Forget it. Oh how I envy you getting away from all this second-rate meandering...

DESMOND: I thought your last love affair would have shocked you into accepting or refusing the conditions — it's queer how we all have to be shocked into a big change, isn't it? Something will have to shock me out of this, or chain me down forever — but perhaps you weren't really in love with Roger Coote...

TOOTS: *(Indignantly.)* I was, frightfully in love with him — you know I was. I only broke off the engagement when I saw how hopeless it was...

DESMOND: It's a good thing you did; the last time I saw him he was being thrown out of somewhere or other for being drunk and disorderly.

TOOTS: Desmond, you are a *beast!*

DESMOND: Sorry, Toots darling. Forgive me. Say you'll forgive me. *(He sits down beside her, and strokes her hair.)* I know your little heart is broken; I know things can never be the same again; I know how hard it is to forget — *but* came Dawn, and with it a great big He-man, with a heavy golden moustache, who'll take you in his arms, and...

TOOTS: *(Tragically.)* You don't know what love is.

DESMOND: *(Coaxing her.)* No, but I know what drink is. Uncle Alfred, Father's younger brother, used to have D.T.'s in this very room — yes, my dear — and he shot himself in the end — in the head, I mean. It was all hushed up, but anyway Roger would have had D.T.'s at least once a week so it's just as well you didn't marry him — the love of a pure woman can do anything *except* wean a man away from the bottle. But I know what I'll do; we'll have a party.

TOOTS: I hate parties.

DESMOND: Not mine. I'm going to be twenty-one tomorrow, so I'll have a party tomorrow night in my Studio, and we'll get very drunk, and forget...

TOOTS: *(Coming round.)* Is it your birthday?

DESMOND: It is. Don't congratulate me, it is not an occasion for congratulation. No, when I've reached fifty and find myself safely anchored in an atmosphere of plush and prosperity, I shall *then* allow you to congratulate me.

TOOTS: Bitter pill, aren't you?

DESMOND: This party tomorrow night is to celebrate the death of my childhood, and farewell to happiness. Rejoice, O young man in thy youth! Who said that? It's a stupid lie. I hate youth. The only happy people I know are doddering peacefully into the grave.

TOOTS: I'll get drunk tomorrow night. What is it like to get drunk, really drunk?

DESMOND: Divine.

TOOTS: Now I know why so many spend their lives in an alcoholic haze.

DESMOND: It will be a beautiful party; everyone will fight; we'll all be miserable — I *love* that!

TOOTS: Ring up the people tonight. There are some Americans arriving tomorrow morning from Poughkeepsie or somewhere. Mother and I are suppose to entertain them — I'll bring the daughter along.

DESMOND: We'll go shares on the drink.

MOONSHINE
by Jim Nolan

MCKEEVER
ELIZABETH

After abruptly leaving her village five years previously, Elizabeth, the vicar's daughter, returns home as her mother lay dying. Her awkward reunion with McKeever, the sometimes undertaker and theatre director, has them at a crossroads similar to that of five years ago.

MCKEEVER: The prodigal daughter....has returned.

ELIZABETH: Hello Mac.

MCKEEVER: Yes. Oh yes. And her name....shall be called Elizabeth.

ELIZABETH: Long time no see. I...I just got back today. Would have called round but I had to go to the hospital. I gather you know about Mum.

MCKEEVER: Yes.

ELIZABETH: Dad wrote to me. I got here as soon as I could.

MCKEEVER: Yes. No news like bad news — as the fella said. Used to be the way with telegrams once. Oh yes, I'm telling you — run like the clappers from the postboy's bike, no good news ever came in a telegram. Not strictly true, of course, but in general. *(Pause.)* And the father. The father. Always on the lookout for them, one step ahead of the posse, waiting for the corpse to come home. Over to Shannon for the American ones, the English came up on the *Princess Maud*. Sometimes I used to go with him for the spin and he'd be singing the whole way home. Singing, if you don't mind. Because he was happy, you see. Only you're not supposed to be! You can't be singing "The Whistling Gypsy" at the head of a funeral, beltin' out an aria on Shop Street, with someone's Auntie Mary in the back of the hearse. No siree, not the ticket. So! Only on the open road where no one could tell him otherwise. *(Pause.)* Yes. Where did that come from?

ELIZABETH: *(Laughing.)* You were talking about telegrams.

MCKEEVER: Telegrams. Yes. Mind if I join you?

ELIZABETH: Of course not.

MCKEEVER: *(Taking a pew opposite her.)* Only I was passing, you see.

My perambulations. And the lights through the colouredy windows catching my eye. Will those who pass this way today a little prayer to Jesus say.

ELIZABETH: It's good to see you, Mac.

MCKEEVER: Yes? You too. Good Friday. He's over the worst now.

ELIZABETH: Who?

MCKEEVER: Jesus. All downhill from here. Sunday's the big day of course. Res-urrection. Lovely word that.

ELIZABETH: You haven't changed much.

MCKEEVER: You have. I can tell. Older.

ELIZABETH: Five years older.

(Pause. She gets up, moves away. Change-the-subject time.)

ELIZABETH: So. How have you been?

MCKEEVER: Never better. *(Sharply.)* And you?

ELIZABETH: I met Michael earlier. He tells me you're still putting on the plays.

MCKEEVER: Still trying to. Nearly there this time though. Sunday night. Parish Hall. No, scrub that. Not now. *(Looking around.)* Somewhere.

ELIZABETH: What are you doing?

MCKEEVER: *A Midsummer Night's Dream.* Thought it might be appropriate.

ELIZABETH: At Easter?

MCKEEVER: Precisely.

ELIZABETH: God, you really haven't changed, have you? *(Lightly.)* No wonder the drama society got rid of you.

MCKEEVER: Philistines. And they didn't get rid of me. I *resigned*.

ELIZABETH: For assaulting Mr. Gibson, I believe.

MCKEEVER: Long overdue. Last time he tells me I'm taking things too seriously.

ELIZABETH: You broke his jaw, Mac — he might have a point.

MCKEEVER: Probation Act applied. Fifty quid in the poor box. No more to be said. *(Pause.)* So what's the answer?

ELIZABETH: What?

MCKEEVER: To *my* question. So, how have you been, says you. Never better, says I. And *you?*

ELIZABETH: *(Laughs.)* Persistent as ever. I'm all right, Mac.

MCKEEVER: What have you been up to? As they say.

ELIZABETH: Not a lot. Got a job. Went to college. Got another job.

Anyway, I explained all that in my letters — to which, of course, you never replied.

MCKEEVER: No. Daddy must have been surprised to see you.

ELIZABETH: He was, a little.

MCKEEVER: And Peggy? That's what they call her above in the hospital. *(Sarcastic.)* Very touching.

ELIZABETH: She didn't recognize me. It would have been nice to say hello.

MCKEEVER: And goodbye.

ELIZABETH: It's as though she were already dead. I'm sure you're familiar with the condition.

MCKEEVER: The death trance. A sort of rehearsal for the real thing.

ELIZABETH: There were things I wanted to tell her. Nothing grandiose or vital or anything. Small things. That I was sorry for what happened to us. That I was well and that I would look after him as best I could. *(Pause.)* Mostly that I would remember her.

MCKEEVER: Gone but not forgotten.

ELIZABETH: What?

MCKEEVER: My father. It's what he used to write on the bill.

ELIZABETH: How is he?

MCKEEVER: Singing probably — in the Heavenly Choir.

ELIZABETH: I'm sorry. I didn't know.

MCKEEVER: The year after you left. Buried him in one of his own coffins. And between you and me — under the breath of course and out of deference to them that didn't know his little secret — I sang! The Bohemian Girl, if I remember correctly — the whole fucking lot. We all have our own way of saying goodbye, y'see.

(Sings.) I dreamt I dwelt in marble halls
With vassals and serfs by my side.
Once upon a time there lived a little town called
Ballintra a man of whom it could be said was neither
plain nor pretty and as happily unhappy as the day is long.

ELIZABETH: I have to go, Mac. Dad will be back from the hospital soon.

MCKEEVER: There lived in that town also a young and very beautiful girl. When she was still a little girl, her father sent her away to the big school in the city. Why, you might ask. He was afraid, I suppose, but that's sometimes the way between the daddies and the daughters.

ELIZABETH: I don't have time for playing games, Mac.

MCKEEVER: It's not a game, it's a fairytale. Every summer the girl would return to the sleepy town, spending her time, for she had lots of it, in the garden of the Big House where she lived or, in the evenings, walking by the seashore. The man, who had little else to do, liked to go there also. Every night, regular as clockwork, up and down the beach he'd go, counting all the white horses or waiting for the sea giants to rise up from the ocean floor and swallow him up. At first he didn't notice the girl and then, when he did, he tried not to, for she was really very young. But then...one evening as he passed her on the beach, the girl smiled at him and he smiled back. That was it. Nothing else, she continued on her way and he on his — but something had happened, the man had become enchanted by the beautiful princess.

ELIZABETH: Get to the point, Mac.

MCKEEVER: I'm trying.

ELIZABETH: I have to go.

MCKEEVER: *Please.* Not yet. I haven't finished my story.

ELIZABETH: I know the end.

MCKEEVER: I don't.

ELIZABETH: The girl was enchanted also. The rector's teenage daughter falls for the balding undertaker. No one knew, but they fell in love and lived happily ever after. Goodnight, Mac — I'll see you tomorrow.

MCKEEVER: Only they didn't. They fell in love all right. As deep as you can fall — but not happily ever after.

ELIZABETH: You can hardly blame me for that.

MCKEEVER: She went away. Gone to London to see the Queen, said the Rector.

ELIZABETH: You're the one who left. I took a boat to England, but it was you who really disappeared.

MCKEEVER: Temporary retreat. Silence of the room. Not easy.

ELIZABETH: I was seventeen. It wasn't easy for me either.

MCKEEVER: Of course not. The two of them. Needed time, that's all. Adjustments. Necessary adjustments.

ELIZABETH: You said you loved me but you couldn't bring yourself to the 'phone.

MCKEEVER: Out of order. Not the 'phone. Me. Our Father who art in exile.

ELIZABETH: Safe in his little room. You didn't even have the courage to tell me why.

MCKEEVER: Implications!

ELIZABETH: What implications?

MCKEEVER: The young girl and the older man.

ELIZABETH: Don't give me that. I knew what I was doing.

MCKEEVER: The man did too — that was the trouble.

ELIZABETH: We were lovers, Mac — it's not a crime.

MCKEEVER: On the contrary — a gift from the gods!

ELIZABETH: Not from the gods — from you. That's what I could never understand. Because you *did* love me, didn't you?

MCKEEVER: Why are you crying, the princess enquired. Because I'm happy, the man replied. Because I love you. *(Pause.)* A long time ago.

ELIZABETH: So bloody happy that he walked away! Oh but not without the thrilling final curtain. No conventional ending for McKeever. The climax played out on the embalming studio trolley. But you were always one for the unexpected, and it was a perfect location for the death blow, wasn't it?

MCKEEVER: *Contrite! The man is contrite! (Silence.)* But it doesn't matter now.

ELIZABETH: No. It doesn't. It can't. As you said — it was a long time ago. I've had to survive you. On my own. That's what your princess has become, Mac — a survivor. *(ELIZABETH exits.)*

MCKEEVER: *(Silence.)* He sent her away. He didn't know why. If the bastard knew why he would have told her. And after she'd gone, the man on the trolley, cold — as fucking death.

PLAYBOY OF THE WESTERN WORLD
by John Millington Synge

CHRISTY

PEGEEN

> *Pegeen, the local girl who first heard and believed Christy's story about murdering his father, now is tired of his ever-expanding narrative. Christy, meanwhile, is still quite nervous about being discovered yet continues to woo Pegeen.*

PEGEEN: *(Imperiously.)* Fling out that rubbish and put them cups away.

(CHRISTY tidies away in great haste.)

PEGEEN: Shove in the bench by the wall.

(He does so.)

PEGEEN: And hang that glass on the nail. What disturbed it at all?

CHRISTY: *(Very meekly.)* I was making myself decent only, and this a fine country for young lovely girls.

PEGEEN: *(Sharply.)* Whisht your talking of girls. *(Goes to counter on right.)*

CHRISTY: Wouldn't any wish to be decent in a place...

PEGEEN: Whisht, I'm saying.

CHRISTY: *(Looks at her face for a moment with great misgivings, then as a last effort takes up a loy, and goes towards her, with feigned assurance.)* It was with a loy the like of that I killed my father.

PEGEEN: *(Still sharply.)* You've told me that story six times since the dawn of day.

CHRISTY: *(Reproachfully.)* It's a queer thing you wouldn't care to be hearing it and them girls after walking four miles to be listening to me now.

PEGEEN: *(Turning round astonished.)* Four miles?

CHRISTY: *(Apologetically.)* Didn't himself say there were only bona fides living in the place?

PEGEEN: It's bona fides by the road they are, but that lot came over the river lepping the stones. It's not three perches when you go like that, and I was down this morning looking on the papers the post-boy does have in his bag. *(With meaning and emphasis.)* For there was great news this day, Christopher Mahon. *(She goes into room on left.)*

CHRISTY: *(Suspiciously.)* Is it news of my murder?

PEGEEN: *(Inside.)* Murder, indeed.

CHRISTY: *(Loudly.)* A murdered da?

PEGEEN: There was not, but a story filled half a page of the hanging of a man. Ah, that should be a fearful end, young fellow, and it worst of all for a man destroyed his da; for the like of him would get small mercies, and when it's dead he is they'd put him in a narrow grave, with cheap sacking wrapping him round, and pour down quicklime on his head, the way you'd see a woman pouring any frish-frash from a cup.

CHRISTY: *(Very miserably.)* Oh, God help me. Are you thinking I'm safe? You were saying at the fall of night I was shut of jeopardy and I here with yourselves.

PEGEEN: *(Severely.)* You'll be shut of jeopardy no place if you go talking with a pack of wild girls the like of them do be walking abroad with the peelers, talking whispers at the fall of night.

CHRISTY: *(With terror.)* And you're thinking they'd tell?

PEGEEN: *(With mock sympathy.)* Who knows, God help you?

CHRISTY: *(Loudly.)* What joy would they have to bring hanging to the likes of me?

PEGEEN: It's queer joys they have, and who knows the thing they'd do, if it'd make the green stones cry itself to think of you swaying and swiggling at the butt of a rope, and you with a fine, stout neck, God bless you! the way you'd be half an hour, in great anguish, getting your death.

CHRISTY: *(Getting his boots and putting them on.)* If there's that terror of them, it'd be best, maybe, I went on wandering like Esau or Cain and Abel on the sides of Neifin or the Erris plain.

PEGEEN: *(Beginning to play with him.)* It would, maybe, for I've heard the circuit judges this place is a heartless crew.

CHRISTY: *(Bitterly.)* It's more than judges this place is a heartless crew. And isn't it a poor thing to be starting again, and I a lonesome fellow will be looking out on women and girls the way the needy fallen spirits do be looking on the Lord?

PEGEEN: What call have you to be that lonesome when there's poor girls walking Mayo in their thousands now?

CHRISTY: *(Grimly.)* It's well you know what call I have. It's well you know its a lonesome thing to be passing small towns with the lights shining sideways when the night is down, or going in strange places with a dog noising before you and a dog noising behind, or drawn to the cities where you'd hear a voice kissing and talking deep love in every shadow of the ditch, and you passing on with an empty, hungry stomach failing from your heart.

PEGEEN: I'm thinking you're an odd man, Christy Mahon. The oddest walking fellow I ever set my eyes on to this hour today.

CHRISTY: Why would any be but odd men and they living lonesome in the world?

PEGEEN: I'm not odd, and I'm my whole life with my father only.

CHRISTY: *(With infinite admiration.)* How would a lovely, handsome woman the like of you be lonesome when all men should be thronging around to hear the sweetness of your voice, and the little infant children should be pestering your steps, I'm thinking, and you walking the roads.

PEGEEN: I'm hard set to know what way a coaxing fellow the like of yourself should be lonesome either.

CHRISTY: Coaxing?

PEGEEN: Would you have me think a man never talked with the girls would have the words you've spoken today? It's only letting on you are to be lonesome, the way you'd get around me now.

CHRISTY: I wish to God I was letting on; but I was lonesome all times, and born lonesome, I'm thinking, as the moon of dawn. *(Going to the door.)*

PEGEEN: *(Puzzled by his talk.)* Well, it's a story I'm not understanding at all why you'd be worse than another, Christy Mahon, and you a fine lad with the great savagery to destroy your da.

CHRISTY: It's little I'm understanding myself, saving only that my heart's scalded this day, and I going off stretching out the earth between us, the way I'll not be waking near you another dawn of the year till the two of us do arise to hope or judgment with the saints of God, and now I'd best be going with my wattle in my hand, for hanging is a poor thing *(Turning to go.)*, and it's little welcome only is left me in this house to-day.

PEGEEN: *(Sharply.)* Christy.

(He turns around.)

Come here to me.

(He goes towards her.)

Lay down that switch and throw some sods on the fire. You're pot-boy in this place, and I'll not have you mitch off from us now.

CHRISTY: You were saying I'd be hanged if I stay.

PEGEEN: *(Quite kindly at last.)* I'm after going down and reading the fearful crimes of Ireland for two weeks or three, and there wasn't a word of your murder. *(Getting up and going over to the counter.)* They've likely not found the body. You're safe so with ourselves.

CHRISTY: *(Astonished, slowly.)* It's making game of me you were *(Following her with fearful joy.)*, and I can stay so, working at your side, and I not lonesome from this mortal day.

PEGEEN: What's to hinder you staying, except the widow woman or the young girls would inveigle you off?

CHRISTY: *(With rapture.)* And I'll have your words from this day filling my ears, and that look is come upon you meeting my two eyes, and I watching you loafing around in the warm sun, or rinsing your ankles when the night is come.

PEGEEN: *(Kindly, but a little embarrassed.)* I'm thinking you'll be a loyal young lad to have working around, and if you vexed me a while since with your leaguing with the girls, I wouldn't give a thraneen for a lad hadn't a mighty spirit in him and gamy heart.

DEIRDRE
by William Butler Yeats

DEIRDRE
CONCHUBAR

> *Conchubar, an old king, found Deirdre when she was a child and,*
> *amazed by her beauty, took her and raised her. One month before*
> *they were to be married, Deidre ran off with Naoise, a young king.*
> *They hid for seven years, when the old king finally promised forgive-*
> *ness. Deirdre does not believe Conchubar, however, and hides a knife*
> *prior to Conchubar's arrival. Immediately preceding this scene, while*
> *Deirdre begs for their lives, Naoise is gagged and abducted behind her back.*

CONCHUBAR: The traitor who has carried off my wife
        No longer lives. Come to my house now, Deirdre,
        For he that called himself your husband's dead.
DEIRDRE: O, do not touch me. Let me go to him. *(Pause.)*
        King Conchubar is right. My husband's dead.
        A single woman is of no account,
        Lacking array of servants, linen cupboards,
        The bacon hanging — and King Conchubar's house
        All ready, too — I'll to King Conchubar's house.
        It is but wisdom to do willingly
        What has to be.
CONCHUBAR: But why are you so calm?
        I thought that you would curse me and cry out,
        And fall upon the ground and tear your hair.
DEIRDRE: *(Laughing.)* You know too much of women to think so;
        Though, if I were less worthy of desire,
        I would pretend as much; but, being myself,
        It is enough that you were master here.
        Although we are so delicately made,
        There's something brutal in us, and we are won
        By those who can shed blood. It was some woman
        That taught you how to woo: but do not touch me:
        I shall do all you bid me, but not yet,
        Because I have to do what's customary.
        We lay the dead out, folding up the hands,

Closing the eyes, and stretching out the feet,
And push a pillow underneath the head,
Till all's in order; and all this I'll do
For Naoise, son of Usna.

CONCHUBAR: It is not fitting.
You are not now a wanderer, but a queen,
And there are plenty that can do these things.

DEIRDRE: *(Motioning CONCHUBAR away.)* No, no. Not yet. I cannot
        be your queen
Till the past's finished, and its debts are paid.
When a man dies, and there are debts unpaid,
 He wanders by the debtor's bed and cries,
"There's so much owing."

CONCHUBAR: You are deceiving me.
You long to look upon his face again.
Why should I give you now to a dead man
That took you from a living? *(He makes a step towards her.)*

DEIRDRE: In good time.
You'll stir me to more passion than he could,
And yet, if you are wise, you'll grant me this:
That I go look upon him that was once
So strong and comely and held his head so high
That women envied me. For I will see him
All blood-bedabbled and his beauty gone.
It's better, when you're beside me in your strength,
That the mind's eye should call up the soiled body,
And not the shape I loved. Look at him, women.
He heard me pleading to be given up,
Although my lover was still living, and yet
He doubts my purpose. I will have you tell him
How changeable all women are; how soon
 Even the best of lovers is forgot
When his day's finished.

CONCHUBAR: No; but I will trust
The strength that you have praised, and not your purpose.

DEIRDRE: *(Almost with a caress.)* It is so small a gift and you will
        grant it
Because it is the first that I have asked.
He has refused. There is no sap in him;

Nothing but empty veins. I thought as much.
He has refused me the first thing I have asked —
Me, me, his wife. I understand him now;
I know the sort of life I'll have with him;
But he must drag me to his house by force.
If he refuses, *(She laughs.)* he shall be mocked by all.
They'll say to one another, "Look at him
That is so jealous that he lured a man
From over sea, and murdered him, and yet
He trembled at the thought of a dead face!"
(She has her hand upon the curtain.)

CONCHUBAR: How do I know that you have not some knife,
And go to die upon his body?

DEIRDRE: Have me searched,
If you would make make so little of your queen.
It may be that I have a knife hid here
Under my dress. Bid one of these dark slaves
To search me for it. *(Pause.)*

CONCHUBAR: Go to your farewells, Queen.

DEIRDRE: Now strike the wire, and sing to it a while,
Knowing that all is happy, and that you know
Within what bride-bed I shall lie this night,
And by what man, and lie close up to him,
For the bed's narrow, and there outsleep the cockcrow.
(She goes behind the curtain.)

FIVE SCENES FOR
TWO WOMEN

RICHARD'S CORK LEG
by Brendan Behan

BAWD I
BAWD II

This scene takes place in an Irish cemetary in 1972. At the top of the scene, the women appear to be serious mourners, but as soon as they sing their irreverent song, they remove their veils and reveal themselves as "Dublin brassers in working gear."

(Two veiled figures can be seen, on each side of a big Celtic cross, in bowed attitudes of what appears to be deep mourning. They weep. Suddenly the group breaks into "The Other Night I Got an Invitation to a Funeral.")

The other night I got an invitation to a funeral,
But much to my discomfort sure the fellow didn't die,
Of course he was dissatisfied at having disappointed us,
And as soon as he apologized we let the thing go by,
The night of the misfortune, he took us down and treated us.
He called a quart of porter for a company of ten,
When some poor chap enquired to know whose money he
was squandering,
The poor chap got his two eyes put in mourning there and
then.
Then Mulrooney struck MacCusker and MacCusker struck
some other one,
And everyone struck anyone, of whom he had a spite,
And Larry Doyle, the cripple, that was sitting doing nothing,
Got a kick that broke his jaw for not indulging in the fight.

BAWD II: Here! Give over! Give over!
BAWD I: Stop it, can't you. No respect. I like a bit of music myself, but there's a time and a place for everything. Not in a cemetery. Yous'll get us barred.
(The girls remove black mourning veils and are revealed as Dublin brassers in working gear.)
BAWD II: That's one place they won't bar us out of, is the graveyard.
BAWD I: They say this is one of the healthiest graveyards in Dublin.

Set on the shore of Dublin Bay. The sea air is very healthy...the ozoon, you know.

BAWD II: And there's a lovely view. *(She points.)* Look — the Wicklow Mountains and Bray Head.

BAWD I: Killiney Strand.

BAWD II: I was had be a man, there. The first time. Lost my virginity. He was the prefect in charge of the Working Girls' Protection Society. He said he'd show what I wasn't to let the boys do to me. It was on an outing.

BAWD I: The sea washes up a lot of wreckage on Killiney Strand.

BAWD II: I wonder if they ever found me maidenhead.

BAWD I: Rose of Lima! Have respect for the dead.

BAWD II: They can't hear us.

BAWD I: This is the high class part of the cemetery. Very superior class of corpse comes here.

BAWD II: Well, how did Crystal Clear get buried in it, and she a whore?

BAWD I: Well, that was before the graveyard was covered by the Forest Lawn credit card.

BAWD II: What's that?

BAWD I: It's a graveyard in California with a few branches. They investigate foreign graveyards to see their dead don't get mixed up with the wrong class of person.

BAWD II: It's a wonder they didn't go to Glasnevin.

BAWD I: They were going to, but it was too full of revolutionaries. They came to Jim Larkin's tomb and they found out he was in Sing Sing...

BAWD II: Is that in Hollywood?

BAWD I: No, it's a jail where they put Larkin for un-Irish American activities. Anyway, these people didn't want their clients mixed up with him, them, so they came out here. They do the corpses up beautiful, drawn, dressed and stuffed.

BAWD II: Stuffed!

BAWD I: They put them in a coffin with a glass front and you can look at them. They keep them in the chapel here. Oh look, there must be someone there. Some beautiful, rich American.

BAWD II: Let's go and have a look at him.

BAWD I: I suppose it'd be no harm.

(They walk to the chapel door and go in. Enter at the back of the

stage two blind men, CRONIN and THE HERO. They wear trench coats, soft hats and black glasses and have blind men's sticks. They cross furtively and exit. BAWD I and BAWD II return from the chapel.)

BAWD II: *(Crosses herself.)* The Lord have mercy on the dead and let per-petual light shine upon them, may they rest in pace.

BAWD I: *(Crosses herself...raises her right hand to her forehead.)* Ah, to hell with him *(Right hand to her breast.)*, the old bastard *(Right hand to her left shoulder.)*, poxy with money *(Right hand to her right shoulder.)*, he can kiss my royal Irish arse now *(Joins her hands.)*. Amen, for all the good his money will do him.

BAWD II: Ah, but he looked beautiful. It's a pity it wasn't a double coffin — I'd have got in beside him.

BAWD I: Have respect for the diseased departed.

BAWD II: I knew a chap that was out with the Irish soldiers fighting in the United Nations, and he says the Turks does that in grave-yards.

BAWD I: Does what?

BAWD II: Does that.

BAWDI: God between us and all harm.

BAWD II: Yes, all the whores in Turkey line up at the cemetery gates for the men to bring them in at night time. On the tombstone. They are flat tombstones, of course.

BAWD I: *(Quickly — to change the subject.)* It's a beautiful view from here. Look at the top of the Sugarloaf.

BAWD II: I was coming down off the top of it with a divinity student and there was a crowd waiting at the bottom to give us a big cheer. They were after being watching us through a telescope. I'd fainted with the climb and he was only giving me artificial respi-ration. The man that was hiring the telescope was charging six-pence a look. "Interesting view of the hills," he called it. Then when we came into view, he increased the fee to half-a-crown a look. He offered us a pound to go back up the hill and give an encore.

BAWD I: *(Impatiently — BAWD II has no respect!)* There's some beautiful tombstones here. *(They walk to a tombstone and look at it.)* Ah, here's one here. Put there by a widow. Only one day married.

BAWD II: A one night stand, like Duffy Circus.

BAWD I: *(Reads.)*
　　We were but one night wed,
　　One night of blessed content,
　　At dawn he died in bed,
　　My darling came and went.
BAWD II: "Came and went"...dear, dear.

AFTER EASTER
by Anne Devlin

GRETA
ELISH

> *Greta, age thirty-seven, has come to the entrance hall of a convent in
> Belfast to speak with her cousin, Elish O'Toole, a nun who is now
> called Sister Bethany. Greta has recently had disturbing visions:
> "Devils! Angels! Voices! Pictures! I even get the smells. The whole
> thing." Until recently, Greta was a mother and teacher in Oxford, but
> she's broken up with her husband, who's been having an affair.*

ELISH: Will you have some tea?

GRETA: Thank you. She's only brought one cup.

ELISH: The tea is for you
   (GRETA receives the cup.)

ELISH: Some rules never change. We don't take tea with visitors.

GRETA: I remember...of course, it wasn't the evening — it was morning — about 5 A.M. A flame appeared in the curtain facing my
   bed. It was growing bright — I was not sleeping or dreaming. I
   wanted to switch on the light beside me, and not taking my eye
   off the flame I reached out for the light switch but I could not
   find it. So I looked away for a second to find the switch, and
   when I looked back, the flame had disappeared. I remember feeling disappointed. Then I put on the light.

ELISH: Why disappointed?

GRETA: Because I knew that if I had lain perfectly still and simply
   watched the flame it would have remained and I might have
   learnt something. As it was I panicked and reached out to find
   the light. I lay for several hours with the light on just gazing at
   the place where the flame had been then I got up around seven
   and opened the curtains. I went down to the kitchen and made a
   cup of tea. I needed to hear some human voices. It was too early
   to call anybody on the telephone. So I turned on the radio —
   there was singing, and then a man's voice said: "Let us pray on
   this Pentecost Sunday..." I am not a religious person. My father is
   an atheist and my husband is a Marxist. And I had ceased to be a
   Catholic so long ago that I had no idea when Pentecost was — I
   still don't.

ELISH: It's the seventh Sunday after Easter. Which is a movable feast. You should remember that much.

GRETA: But I'm not a believer. And yet that flame — hung there at the foot of my bed in a strange room. At lunchtime I called my husband, he came to collect me. I never spent another night in that house. I don't know why this is happening to me or what I'm supposed to do about it.

ELISH: Where was the house?

GRETA: I told you — in the country. Porlock.

ELISH: I take it that this is not an isolated incident.

GRETA: It's not an isolated incident.

ELISH: Why were you alone at that time?

GRETA: I was unhappy. My husband didn't want children and I did. It was the third strange experience of my life.

(ELISH encourages her to continue.)

GRETA: The second had occurred earlier in the year; on 2 February.

ELISH: The purification.

GRETA: We had some people in to dinner and I was relighting the candles on the table, which had burnt down and gone out. As I moved the candle to the fireplace and reached into the fire and then transferred the lit candles to the stand — the flame leapt. It lit up my hair, which at the time was long and I suddenly found myself surrounded by a curtain of flame.

ELISH: Who put the flames out?

GRETA: What — oh, my husband.

ELISH: How?

GRETA: He took my hair in his hand and beat it. *(She claps.)* Like that. A strange cry came out of my mouth — when the fire caught — it was almost as startling as the fire itself.

ELISH: What did it sound like?

GRETA: *(Chants.)* Ah ah ah ah ah ah. *(She makes a beautiful sound, echoing the nuns singing at the beginning.)*

ELISH: And there was another incident? You said there were three.

GRETA: Yes, the first. For three days before my birthday — in November 1981 — I couldn't sleep. This made me very tired and I became delirious enough to believe that the sleeping bag which I insisted on sleeping in on the floor of my room was the womb and I had gone back into it to be born again. There is hardly any point in stressing again that I am not a religious person and I feel somewhat ashamed of these manifestations.

ELISH: Then why tell me — why not speak with a doctor?

GRETA: If I tell a doctor I am having religious visions, he will tell me that I am ill; and that is closure. If I tell a nun I am having religious visions than we can agree we are both ill and at least begin the conversation on an equal footing.

ELISH: You are aware that I am Prioress here now?

GRETA: I wasn't but I'm glad of it. For at least it means you have the spiritual authority to advise me. You see I don't intend being locked up for what one half of the world regards an achievement of sanctity. My liberty is very important to me...Also —

ELISH: Also?

GRETA: I haven't finished. I was aware during the experience of being in the womb on my birthday, my twenty-fourth birthday, that I could see out of two separate windows each with a different view. I felt very far down inside my own body. As I looked around the room, I saw an old man in the corner watching me. And I said to myself I knew it. I knew that old man was there. I have felt watched all my life.

ELISH: It was the devil you saw.

GRETA: I knew that immediately. He looked like an old priest.

(ELISH makes a movement.)

GRETA: He was dressed like a priest in a long black soutane. He had a pointed beard. I must have been weak and small because I was looking around what I took to be the edge of a chair, a wing chair, or perhaps it was a pram hood. At any rate, the old priest loomed over me and placed a pillow on my face. I tried to cry out but he was smothering me. I was being silenced. And it was this I had to struggle against. I struggled against this smothering blackness until a voice said in my ear — a kind warm voice: "Turn round. You have to turn around." So I did, I turned myself around and found I could breathe again and ahead of me I could see this oh most beautiful globe, a sphere lit up in space far below me, and I found myself floating falling towards it. And the same voice, the one that told me to turn around, said: "Enjoy your fall through space and time." So I knew I was born that night. Or I was reliving my birth.

ELISH: And that was all?

GRETA: All? That was the beginning. Then the hair catching fire, then the flame in the curtain.

ELISH: Have you ever told anyone about this?

GRETA: Not a living soul — except my husband. I did tell him about the flame — when he came to pick me up from the cottage.

ELISH: What did he say?

GRETA: I was very stupid. I told him I'd seen a tongue of fire, and I discovered it was Pentecost Sunday. Stupid!

ELISH: What was his reaction?

GRETA: I lost him...He was repelled — what would you expect? He was a Marxist historian. He thought he'd found a radical secular emancipated woman, and instead he'd got a Catholic mystic.

ELISH: Then why did you tell him? You could have come to me then!

GRETA: I told him because I wanted him to talk me out of it, I suppose. But he didn't even try. Later my husband told me he was having an affair. We went away to try to talk about it. We were staying in a house in Exmoor. And I died.

ELISH: You died?

GRETA: And in my grief my voice left me. I experienced my own death.

ELISH: Why didn't you speak out before?

GRETA: I couldn't, I was afraid. I loved my husband and I had no context for dealing with this. So I shut it in another room and I lived in the outer room of my life I suppose. You see, after we came back from Exmoor, I deliberately got pregnant. So he couldn't leave me. That was what I did. That was my response!

ELISH: Why now? Why are you telling it now? Something has happened to make you speak out!

GRETA: Two nights ago at my sister's flat in London, a figure burst in on me. Stood there beseeching, wailing, shivering at the foot of my bed. I pretended it was a banshee. But it was no more a banshee than I am. We both know what I saw. Why are you crying?

ELISH: The light is hurting my eyes. Excuse me. *(She gets up to blow her nose and wipe her eyes.)*

GRETA: I kept it away for so long. I want to get this under control. Help me! You are crying.

ELISH: You should have been a nun.

GRETA: It's a bit late now. Have you any more practical advice?

ELISH: My mother was a woman of great sanctity. But instead of entering a convent which she ought to have done she married a worthless man with a handsome face who led her a merry dance.

GRETA: A merry dance? He tried to strangle her — was what I was told.

ELISH: After I was born she went away to England, and I was left in the care of your mother. Until she got herself on her feet.

GRETA: On her feet? She got married again.

ELISH: A kind man who fell in love with her and proposed, before he knew about the baby in Belfast.

GRETA: And then you popped up.

ELISH: She told him she had a baby — me. And he still married her. So after ten months of marriage I was brought home to my mother in England. I'm supposed to look like him, the man who tried to strangle my mother. Did you know that? I'm his spitting image. I never really fitted in. And I was sent away to school. To be brought up by nuns. And I have been with nuns ever since. They didn't mind what I looked like — in fact my body wasn't important at all. I knew from the beginning this was how I would live, I felt safe and cared for. And I like the order and the convent routine. I have strived for grace and revelation. I have followed every rule, I have read every text — and I love it here, don't misunderstand this — a convent is a republic of letters. I love the language, the structure, the ceremony, but I have never ever had a revelation such as you describe. I have fasted in Lent. I have lain awake for nights on end to achieve this state of grace that you so artlessly fall into. You and my mother share this — you are effortlessly and unconsciously almost always in a state of grace. They say that Mary Magdalene is the most sanctified woman in heaven. And I who have broken myself on the feet of the Redeemer — *(She indicates a purple-draped figure which is hanging above them in the hall.)* — am rewarded with this visit — and you ask me why I am crying? Did you come here to make fun of me?

GRETA: I have no wish to cast ridicule on your way of life, Elish.

ELISH: Bethany!

GRETA: I came here because I grant that your spiritual practices might give me some insight into my condition. I rather hoped you would open a door for me — which would allow me to live in the main room of my life. But I see you have only caused you distress, I'm sorry —

SIVE
by John B. Keane

SIVE
MENA

> *Sive, a young woman (18) of illegittimate birth, has never been told the full story of her father and mother. She lives with her maternal grandmother, uncle and aunt by marriage; and that aunt has conspired with the local matchmaker to wed Sive to a wealthy old farmer. The aunt, Mena, also wants the grandmother to move out when Sive marries. But Sive resists.*

SIVE: *(Hesitant.)* The tubes of the bicycle are full of holes.
(Mena dries her hands on her apron and turns to Sive.)
MENA: *(Sympathetically.)* We will have to do something about it, for sure. I will tell himself to be on the look for a pair of new tubes in the village. Will I wet a mouthful o' tea for you while you're waiting for the dinner. *(Sive is too surprised to reply.)* There is a piece of sweet cake I have put away. You must be tired after your day.
SIVE: *(Befuddled.)* No...no...don't bother with the tea! I'll wait until the dinner.
MENA: A cup of milk, so! (*Without waiting for reply, she hurries to dresser, takes a cup, fills it and forces it on Sive.*) It must be an ease for you to get away from the nuns and the books, but sure we won't have much more of the schooling now.
(Gently Mena forces Sive to a chair near the table. Sive places the cup before her and looks bewilderedly at Mena at the word "school.")
MENA: Any of the girls in the parish would give their right hand to have the chance that's before you.
SIVE: But...
MENA: *(Quickly before Sive can reply.)* Don't think about it now. Think of the handling of thousands and the fine clothes and perfumery. Think of the hundreds of pounds in Creamery cheques that will come in the door to you and the servant boy and the servant girl falling all over you for fear you might dirty your hands with work.

SIVE: *(Shakes her head several times as though to ward off Mena's words.)* You don't know...you...you...

MENA: Sit down now and rest yourself. You could have your grand-mother with you. Think of the joy it would give the poor woman to have the run of such a fine house...and to see you settled there. 'Tis a fine thing for you, my girl and sure, what matter if he's a few years older than you. Won't we be all old in a handful of short years? Ah! I would give my right hand to be in your shoes.

SIVE: *(Shakes her head continually.)* Please, please...you don't know what you are saying. How can you ask me such a thing?

MENA: Now, tomorrow himself will call to the Convent and tell the Reverend Mother that you will not be going in any more. What would a grown-up woman like you want with spending your days in the middle of children.

SIVE: I could never live with that old man. *(Entreats Mena.)* Fancy the thought of waking in the light of day and looking at him with the small head of him. Oh, my God! No! I could never!...I could not even think of it!

MENA: *(Still motherly.)* Nonsense, child! That is nothing. Have sense for yourself. I know what you are going into. Do you think I would not gainsay him if it wasn't the best thing for you. *(Places a hand around Sive's shoulder.)* Sit here, child, and drink your milk. *(Mena gently brings Sive to the chair, seats her and stands behind her with both hands resting lightly on Sive's shoulders. Mena's face becomes shrewd. Sive looks vacantly before her — towards the audience.)*

MENA: Will you picture yourself off to the chapel every Sunday in your motorcar with your head in the air and you giving an odd look out of the window at the poor oinsheacs in their donkey-and-cars and their dirty oul' shawls and their faces yellow with the dirt by them. Will you thank God that you won't be for the rest of your days working for the bare bite and sup like the poor women of these parts.

SIVE: *(Raises her head and entwines her hands.)* Imagine what the girls at school would say! Imagine going to a dance with him, or going up the chapel with him!

MENA: All I know is that you will be independent. You will have no enemy when you have the name of money.

SIVE: I don't know what to think or say. I do not want to give offence, but I will never marry such a man. I will not marry at all!

MENA: *(Motherly again.)* You will change! You will change when you think by yourself of the misery you are leaving; when you think of the way you were born.

(Sive eagerly turns and looks innocently at Mena. She is changed suddenly to an eager girl awaiting the solution to a problem that has for a long time baffled her.)

SIVE: Surely you don't remember when I was born. *(Her eyes widen as she looks at Mena. For the first time she takes an interest in Mena's soliloquy.)* Nobody ever told me about my father or mother or what sort of people they were.

(Sive looks into Mena's face searching for the truth.)

MENA: I will tell the tale. Himself would never bring himself to say it. You would think it was some kind of a blemish that should be hidden and sure, what was it, only the work of nature. Your mother, God grant her a bed in heaven, was a nice lie of a girl. Your father took himself away quickly out of these parts and, if he is alive, never made himself known. There was no blame to your mother, God help her. Your grandmother, for all yeer talking and whispering behind my back, was never the one to come out with the truth.

SIVE: But my father...wasn't he drowned in England?

MENA: Your father was never a father, God forgive him. He straightened his sails and disappeared like the mist of a May morning. It was no wonder your mother died with the shame of it. No blame, achree! *(With feeling then.)* No blame to what is mortal. Do you think it is how two people will stay apart forever who have blood becoming a flood in their veins. It is the way things happen...*(Conviction.)*...the sound of fiddles playing airy hornpipes, the light of a moon on the pale face of a river, the whispered word...the meeting of soft arms and strong arms...*(Pauses.)* ...

SIVE: I thought you said you'd tell me about my father.

MENA: *(Unaccountably vexed.)* I'm telling you. Your father was nothing. He was no father. He had no name. You have no name. You will have no name till you take a husband. Do you see the hungry greyhound or the mongrel dog? It is the same way with a man. It is no more than the hunger. It is time you were told, my girl. You are a bye-child, a common bye-child — a bastard!

(Sive attempts to rise. Mena roughly pushes her back in the chair.)

MENA: You will sleep with that old woman no longer. *(She flings the schoolbag across the room.)* There will be no more school for you. School is a place for schoolmasters and children. Every woman will come to the age when she will have a mind for a room of her own. I mind when I was a child, when I was a woman, there were four sisters of us in the one room. There was no corner of a bed we could call our own. We used to sit into the night talking and thieving and wondering where the next ha'penny would come from or thinking would it ever come to our turn to meet a boy that we might go with, and be talking with and maybe make a husband out of. We would kill. *(Vexed.)* We would beg, borrow or steal. We would fire embers of fire at the devil to leave the misery of our own house behind us, to make a home with a man, any man that would show four walls to us for his time in the world. *(In a voice of warning.)* Take no note of the man who has nothing to show for himself, who will be full of rameish and bladder, who would put wings on ould cows for you but has no place to make a marriage bed for you. Take heed of a man with a piece of property. He will stand over his promise. He will keep the good word for you because he has the keeping of words... Now go to the room and be sure to think of what I said.

(Sive rises instinctively goes towards her own room but remembering, turns and exits by the far door to Mena's bedroom.)

YOUTH'S THE SEASON
by Mary Manning

Toots
Connie

Connie Millington and Toots have been left to talk in the Millington drawing room. Connie has been seeing Terence Killigrew — a wit, a writer, and a scoundrel.

CONNIE: *(Combing her hair nervously.)* I look terrible — grey and old and shattered, and that awful Harry will be here at any moment. Now Toots, what do you want to talk to me about?

TOOTS: *(Thoughtfully.)* When are you going to give up Terence?

CONNIE: *(Pausing.)* What do you mean?

TOOTS: You heard me, darling. When are you going to give up Terence and marry Harry Middleton?

CONNIE: How do you know I won't marry Terence?

TOOTS: Because — to be quite brutal — he won't marry you.

CONNIE: Thanks. And since you're so certain about everything what makes you think that Harry wants to marry me?

TOOTS: Snap out of it! The man is besotted. He exudes honourable intentions. He's probably asked you already, but you're so infatuated by this drunken egotistical loafer...

CONNIE: *(Swinging round.)* I won't allow you to speak about Terence like that. He's got genius. He's worth a hundred Harry Middletons.

TOOTS: We shall see. So you think you can reform Terence? Oh, Connie, take it from me, it can't be done.

CONNIE: Because you failed, it doesn't say I'll fail.

TOOTS: Ah, you're bound to fail. You haven't enough brains; you haven't enough guts; you're selfish and flabby; you'd never pull that job through. I couldn't, and I'm twice the man you are.

CONNIE: Go on, call me names — anything else?

TOOTS: Plenty. It would need a strong woman to pull Terence out of the morass he is in, and keep him out; you're not strong enough, my dear — no, you'll do very nicely behind the mosquito nets in Kenya surrounded by pots of cold cream and all the latest novels from England.

CONNIE: Shut up! Shut up!

TOOTS: Terence is beyond hope. He's degenerate, decadent, effete, and rotten. Leave him alone.

CONNIE: *(Almost shouting at her.)* I'll show you — I'll show you. I can pull him together — I can do it...I'll marry him.

TOOTS: *(Calmly.)* Has this man ever told you he loves you?

CONNIE: *(Hesitating.)* Not in so many words.

TOOTS: Only three are necessary.

CONNIE: But I know he does instinctively.

TOOTS: If you're so certain of Terence, why keep Harry hanging on?

CONNIE: Physically he's attractive enough — and he's useful...

TOOTS: As a whip to spur on Terence. Poor Connie, it won't work, not with that selfish egoist. Well I must be off...

CONNIE: No, don't go...oh Toots, I'm so miserable. *(She sits down on the sofa.)*

TOOTS: Of course you are. You simply won't look facts in the face. Even if Terence loved you...

CONNIE: *(Whimpering.)* He does love me — it's simply his financial position —

TOOTS: My dear girl, he hasn't got a financial position. He was obviously borrowing from his unfortunate pimply brother this morning; he'll never be able to marry.

CONNIE: *(Sobbing.)* He has a future, I know he has — he's writing a novel. Damn! Now I've gone and spoiled my makeup.

TOOTS: And so you think you're going to be his inspiration — his helpmate — Oh, Connie, if only you didn't imagine yourself an intellectual.

CONNIE: *(Sniffing.)* I am intellectual. *(Defiantly.)* I've read *Ulysses* through twice!

TOOTS: Only for pornographic pickings.

CONNIE: You're horribly unsympathetic, and it's no use advising me. I want Terence, and I mean to have him. Do leave me — no, don't go. *(She sobs hysterically.)* Oh God, I don't know what to do — Oh, I'm so miserable, I don't know what to do...

TOOTS: *(Sternly.)* Now Connie, I am sympathetic; I am really, it's only I can see the hell you're heading for...

BAILEGANGAIRE

by Tom Murphy

DOLLY
MARY

> *Dolly, thirty-nine, a louche and not exactly happily married woman with many children, visits with her sister Mary, forty-one and a spinster who cares for their senile grandmother. In this scene Dolly, pregnant again, makes a proposition.*

DOLLY: She's asleep! Mommo!...She's asleep, it's ten to ten. Ten to ten, 1984, and I read it — how long ago was it? — that by 1984 we'd all be going on our holidays to the moon in *Woman's Own*.

MARY: She's not asleep.

DOLLY: I'm not arg'in' about it. She's — resting.

MARY: And I'm going to rouse her again in a minute. You were saying?

DOLLY: *(Stretching herself, flaunting her stomach.)* And a telly would fit nicely over there.

MARY: A plan, a proposition, you have it all figured out?

DOLLY: And I'm sorry now I spent the money on the video. No one uses it. You'd make more use of it. It has a remote. *(In answer to Mary's query "remote.")* Yeh know? One of them things yeh — *(Holds in her hand.)* — and — *(Further demonstrates.)* — control.

MARY: I have a video here already. Mommo. What's your plan?

DOLLY: Wait'll we have a drink. She's guilty.

MARY: Guilty of what?

DOLLY: I don't know.

MARY: Then why —

DOLLY: I'm not arg'in' with yeh. *(Offering to top up Mary's drink.)*

MARY: Why can't you ever finish a subject or talk straight? I don't want another drink.

DOLLY: I'm talking straight.

MARY: What's on your mind, Dolly? I'm up to you.

DOLLY: There's no one up to Dolly.

MARY: Tck!

DOLLY: I'm talkin' straight!

(Another car passes by outside.)

DOLLY: Traffic. The weekend-long meeting at the computer plant place. And all the men, busy, locked outside the fence.

MARY: *(Abrupt movement to the table.)* On second thoughts. *(And pours lemonade into her glass.)*

DOLLY: *(Is a bit drunk now and getting drunker.)* No, wait a minute.

MARY: What-are-you-saying, Dolly?

DOLLY: An' that's why she goes on like a gramophone. Guilty.

MARY: This is nonsense.

DOLLY: And so are you.

MARY: So am I!

DOLLY: An' you owe me a debt.

MARY: What do I owe you?

DOLLY: And she had to get married.

MARY: *(To herself.)* Impossible.

DOLLY: No! No! — Mary? No. Wait a minute —

MARY: *(Fingers to her forehead.)* Dolly, I'm —

DOLLY: I'm talkin' straight.

MARY: Trying to get a grip of — Ahmm. I'm trying to find — ahmm. Get control of — ahmm. My life, Dolly.

DOLLY: Yes. You're trying to say, make head and tail of it all, talk straight, like myself. No, Mary, hold on! You told me one thing, I'll tell you another. D'yeh remember the pony-and-trap-Sunday-outings? I don't. But I remember — now try to contradict this — the day we buried Grandad. Now I was his favourite so I'll never forget it. And whereas — No, Mary! — whereas! She stood there over that hole in the ground like a rock — like a duck, like a duck, her chest stickin' out. Not a tear.

MARY: What good would tears have been?

DOLLY: Not a tear. And — And! — Tom buried in that same hole in the ground a couple of days before. Not a tear, then or since. *(Wandering to the table for another drink.)* Oh I gathered a few "newses" about our Mommo.

MARY: Maybe she's crying now.

DOLLY: All of them had to get married except myself and Old Sharp Eyes. Mrs. McGrath the sergeant said. But she bore a bastard all the same. Her Stephen. *(Wanders to the radio and switches it off.)* The hypocrite.

MARY: Leave it on.

DOLLY: I've a proposition.

MARY: It's the Sunday Concert. Switch it on.

DOLLY: *(Switches on the radio.)* So what d'yeh think?

MARY: About what?

DOLLY: The slated *(Gestures roof.)* the other things I mentioned.

MARY: It would stop the place falling down for someone alright.

DOLLY: An' half of this place is mine, I'll sign it over.

MARY: To whom?

DOLLY: To whom. To Jack-Paddy-Andy, to Kitty-the-Hare, to you. And there might be — other things — you might need.

MARY: What else could anyone need?

(Dolly now looking a bit hopeless, pathetic, offering a cigarette to Mary, lighting it for Mary.)

DOLLY: An' would you like another? *(Drinks. Mary shakes her head.)* Lemonade?

MARY: No. What are you trying to say?

DOLLY: An' the turf out there won't last the winter.

MARY: You said that.

DOLLY: And one of the children.

(She looks at Mary for a reaction. But all this time Mary's mind, or half of it, is on Mommo.) Yeh. Company for yeh.

MARY: I get all this if I stay.

DOLLY: Or go.

MARY: *(Becoming more alert.)* What?...You want me to go? With one of the children?...Which one of the children?

DOLLY: *(Continues with closed eyes through the following.)* Jesus, I'm tired. A brand new one. *(Mary laughs incredulously.)* Would you? Would you? Would you?

MARY: What?

DOLLY: Take him. It.

MARY: With me?

DOLLY: *(Nods.)* An' no one need be any the wiser.

MARY: And if I stay?

DOLLY: Say it's yours. It'll all blow over in a month.

MARY: You're crazy.

DOLLY: That makes three of us. I'm not crazy. I'm — as you can see.

MARY: Yes, I've wondered for some time, but I thought you couldn't — you couldn't! — be that stupid. *(A car passes by outside.)*

DOLLY: More take-aways for the lads. *(She starts wearily for her coat.)* My, but they're busy.

MARY: No one is asking you to leave.

DOLLY: *(Stops. Eyes closed again.)* You'll be paid.

MARY: I've heard you come up with a few things before, but!

DOLLY: Stephen'll kill me.

MARY: What about me?

DOLLY: Or he'll cripple me.

MARY: Do you ever think of others!

DOLLY: Or I'll fix him.

MARY: And you'll be out — gallivanting — again tomorrow night.

DOLLY: And the night after, and the night after. And you can be sure of that.

MARY: How long are you gone?

DOLLY: Six, seven months.

MARY: Six, seven months.

DOLLY: Trying to conceal it.

MARY: Who's the father?

DOLLY: I have my suspicions.

MARY: But he's busy perhaps tonight, picketing?

DOLLY: Yes, very busy. Travelling at the sound of speed. But the Chinese'll get them. *(Opens her eyes.)* Hmm?

MARY: And this is the help? This is what you've been figuring out?

DOLLY: You can return the child after, say, a year. If you want to.

MARY: I thought your figuring things out were about —? *(She indicates Mommo. Then she goes to Mommo.)* Mommo, open your eyes, time to continue.

DOLLY: After a year it'll be easy to make up a story.

MARY: Another story! *(She laughs.)*

DOLLY: You're a nurse, you could help me if you wanted to.

MARY: Trying all my life to get out of this situation and now you want to present me with the muddle of your stupid life to make sure the saga goes on.

DOLLY: Oh the saga will go on.

MARY: Mommo!

DOLLY: I'll see to that, one way or the other.

MARY: *(To herself.)* I go away with a brand new baby. Mommo! *(To Dolly.)* Where? Where do I go? *(Dolly nods.)* You have that figured out too?

DOLLY: We can discuss that.

(Mary laughs.)

DOLLY: You're its aunt.

MARY: Its! *(She laughs.)*

DOLLY: Aunt! — Aunt! — And you're a nurse! — Aunt!

MARY: Mommo! I know you're not asleep.

DOLLY: *(Shrugs.)* OK. *(Now talking to herself.)* And if it's a boy you can call it Tom, and if it's a girl you can call it Tom.

FOUR SCENES FOR
TWO MEN

WAITING FOR GODOT
by Samuel Beckett

ESTRAGON
VLADIMIR

> *Vladimir (Didi) and Estragon (Gogo) have been waiting near a tree for Godot, whose arrival has been promised by a young boy. While waiting, Vladimir and Estragon have been visited by Pozzo and Lucky, they've parted ways and rejoined, and Estragon has been beaten up overnight — again.*

(Estragon sleeps. Vladimir gets up softly, takes off his coat and lays it across Estragon's shoulders, then starts walking up and down, swinging his arms to keep himself warm. Estragon wakes with a start, jumps up, casts about wildly. Vladimir runs to him, puts his arms around him.)

VLADIMIR: There...there...Didi is there...don't be afraid...

ESTRAGON: Ah!

VLADIMIR: There...there...it's all over...

ESTRAGON: I was falling —

VLADIMIR: It's all over, it's all over.

ESTRAGON: I was on top of a —

VLADIMIR: Don't tell me! Come, we'll walk it off. *(He takes Estragon by the arm and walks him up and down until Estragon refuses to go any further.)*

ESTRAGON: That's enough. I'm tired.

VLADIMIR: You'd rather be stuck there doing nothing?

ESTRAGON: Yes.

VLADIMIR: Please yourself. *(He releases Estragon, picks up his coat and puts it on.)*

ESTRAGON: Let's go.

VLADIMIR: We can't.

ESTRAGON: Why not?

VLADIMIR: We're waiting for Godot.

ESTRAGON: Ah! *(Vladimir walks up and down.)* Can you not stay still?

VLADIMIR: I'm cold.

ESTRAGON: We came too soon.

VLADIMIR: It's always at nightfall.

ESTRAGON: But night doesn't fall.

VLADIMIR: It'll fall all of a sudden, like yesterday.

ESTRAGON: Then it'll be night.

VLADIMIR: And we can go.

ESTRAGON: Then it'll be day again. *(Pause. Despairing.)* What'll we do, what'll we do!

VLADIMIR: *(Halting, violently.)* Will you stop whining? I've had about my bellyful of your lamentations!

ESTRAGON: I'm going.

VLADIMIR: *(Seeing Lucky's hat.)* Well!

ESTRAGON: Farewell.

VLADIMIR: Lucky's hat. *(He goes towards it.)* I've been here an hour and never saw it. *(Very pleased.)* Fine!

ESTRAGON: You'll never see me again.

VLADIMIR: I knew it was the right place. Now our troubles are over. *(He picks up the hat, contemplates it, straightens it.)* Must have been a very fine hat. *(He puts it on in place of his own which he hands to Estragon.)* Here.

ESTRAGON: What?

VLADIMIR: Hold that.

(Estragon takes Vladimir's hat. Vladimir adjusts Lucky's hat on his head. Estragon puts on Vladimir's hat in place of his own which he hands to Vladimir. Vladimir takes Estragon's hat. Estragon adjusts Vladimir's hat on his head. Vladimir puts on Estragon's hat in place of Lucky's which he hands to Estragon. Estragon takes Lucky's hat. Vladimir adjusts Estragon's hat on his head. Estragon puts on Lucky's hat in place of Vladimir's which he hands to Vladimir. Vladimir takes his hat. Estragon adjusts Lucky's on his head. Estragon puts on his hat in place of Lucky's which he hands to Vladimir. Vladimir takes Lucky's hat. Estragon adjusts his hat on his head. Vladimir puts on Lucky's hat in place of his own which he hands to Estragon. Estragon takes Vladimir's hat. Vladimir adjusts Lucky's hat on his head. Estragon hands Vladimir's hat back to Vladimir who takes it and hands it back to Estragon who takes it and hands it back to Vladimir who takes it and throws it down.)

VLADIMIR: How does it fit me?

ESTRAGON: How would I know?

VLADIMIR: No, but how do I look in it? *(He turns his head coquettishly to and fro, minces like a mannequin.)*

ESTRAGON: Hideous.

VLADIMIR: Yes, but not more so than usual?

ESTRAGON: Neither more nor less.

VLADIMIR: Then I can keep it. Mine irked me. *(Pause.)* How shall I say? *(Pause.)* It itched me. *(He takes off Lucky's hat, peers into it, shakes it, knocks on the crown, puts it on again.)*

ESTRAGON: I'm going. *(Silence.)*

VLADIMIR: Will you not play?

ESTRAGON: Play at what?

VLADIMIR: We could play at Pozzo and Lucky.

ESTRAGON: Never heard of it.

VLADIMIR: I'll do Lucky, you do Pozzo. *(He imitates Lucky sagging under the weight of his baggage. Estragon looks at him with stupefaction.)* Go on.

ESTRAGON: What am I to do?

VLADIMIR: Curse me!

ESTRAGON: *(After reflection.)* Naughty!

VLADIMIR: Stronger!

ESTRAGON: Gonococcus! Spirochete! *(Vladimir sways back and forth, doubled in two.)*

VLADIMIR: Tell me to think.

ESTRAGON: What?

VLADIMIR: Say, Think, pig!

ESTRAGON: Think, pig! *(Silence.)*

VLADIMIR: I can't!

ESTRAGON: That's enough of that.

VLADIMIR: Tell me to dance.

ESTRAGON: I'm going.

VLADIMIR: Dance, hog! *(He writhes. Exit Estragon left, precipitately.)* I can't! *(He looks up, misses Estragon.)* Gogo! *(He moves wildly about the stage. Enter Estragon left, panting. He hastens towards Vladimir, falls into his arms.)* There you are again at last!

ESTRAGON: I'm accursed!

VLADIMIR: Where were you? I thought you were gone for ever.

ESTRAGON: They're coming!

VLADIMIR: Who?

ESTRAGON: I don't know.

VLADIMIR: How many?

ESTRAGON: I don't know.

VLADIMIR: *(Triumphantly.)* It's Godot! At last! Gogo! It's Godot! We're saved! Let's go and meet him! *(He drags Estragon towards the wings. Estragon resists, pulls himself free, exit right.)* Gogo! Come back! *(Vladimir runs to extreme left, scans the horizon. Enter Estragon right, he hastens towards Vladimir, falls into his arms.)* There you are again again!

ESTRAGON: I'm in hell!

VLADIMIR: Where were you?

ESTRAGON: They're coming there too!

VLADIMIR: We're surrounded! *(Estragon makes a rush towards back.)* Imbecile! There's no way out there. *(He takes Estragon by the arm and drags him towards front. Gesture towards front.)* There! Not a soul in sight! Off you go! Quick! *(He pushes Estragon towards auditorium. Estragon recoils in horror.)* You won't? *(He contemplates auditorium.)* Well I can understand that. Wait till I see. *(He reflects.)* Your only hope left is to disappear.

ESTRAGON: Where?

VLADIMIR: Behind the tree. *(Estragon hesitates.)* Quick! Behind the tree. *(Estragon goes and crouches behind the tree, realizes he is not hidden, comes out from behind the tree.)* Decidedly this tree will not have been the slightest use to us.

ESTRAGON: *(Calmer.)* I lost my head. Forgive me. It won't happen again. Tell me what to do.

VLADIMIR: There's nothing to do.

ESTRAGON: You go and stand there. *(He draws Vladimir to extreme right and places him with his back to the stage.)* There, don't move, and watch out. *(Vladimir scans horizon, screening his eyes with his hand. Estragon runs and takes up same position extreme left. They turn their heads and look at each other.)* Back to back like in the good old days. *(They continue to look at each other for a moment, then resume their watch. Long silence.)* Do you see anything coming?

VLADIMIR: *(Turning his head.)* What?

ESTRAGON: *(Louder.)* Do you see anything coming?

VLADIMIR: No.

ESTRAGON: Nor I. *(They resume their watch. Silence.)*

VLADIMIR: You must have had a vision.

ESTRAGON: *(Turning his head.)* What?

VLADIMIR: *(Louder.)* You must have had a vision.

ESTRAGON: No need to shout! *(They resume their watch. Silence.)*

VLADIMIR: *(Turning simultaneously.)* Do you —

ESTRAGON: Do you —

VLADIMIR: Oh pardon!

ESTRAGON: Carry on.

VLADIMIR: No, no after you.

ESTRAGON: No, no, you first.

VLADIMIR: I interrupted you.

ESTRAGON: On the contrary. *(They glare at each other angrily.)*

VLADIMIR: Ceremonious ape!

ESTRAGON: Punctilious pig!

VLADIMIR: Finish your phrase, I tell you!

ESTRAGON: Finish your own! *(Silence. They draw closer, halt.)*

VLADIMIR: Moron!

ESTRAGON: That's the idea, let's abuse each other. *(They turn, move apart, turn again and face each other.)*

VLADIMIR: Moron!

ESTRAGON: Vermin!

VLADIMIR: Abortion!

ESTRAGON: Morpion!

VLADIMIR: Sewer-rat!

ESTRAGON: Curate!

VLADIMIR: Cretin!

ESTRAGON: *(With finality.)* Crritic!

VLADIMIR: Oh! *(He wilts, vanquished, and turns away.)*

ESTRAGON: Now let's make it up.

VLADIMIR: Gogo!

ESTRAGON: Didi!

VLADIMIR: Your hand!

ESTRAGON: Take it!

VLADIMIR: Come to my arms!

ESTRAGON: Your arms?

VLADIMIR: My breast!

ESTRAGON: Off we go! *(They embrace. They separate. Silence.)*

VLADIMIR: How time flies when one has fun! *(Silence.)*

ESTRAGON: What do we do now?
VLADIMIR: While waiting.
ESTRAGON: While waiting.
(Silence.)

FORTY-FOUR SYCAMORE
by Bernard Farrell

VINNY

DEREK

Vinny, twenty-three, and his wife Joan have invited Derek, twenty-seven, and his wife for cocktails in a suburban development carved out of an old estate. Vinny's plan to make friends and professional contacts is upset by two things: Derek and Hilary have come expecting a dinner which doesn't exist and Joan has invited Mr. Prentice, an elderly man suspected of peering in bedroom windows. Vinny and Mr. Prentice have just forcefully squared off over the future of the remaining estate and Vinny's plan to sell security systems. Prentice now lies immobile throughout the scene.

VINNY: What did you just say? How did you know about that?

DEREK: Know about what?

VINNY: *(Angrily.)* I'm talking to you, Prentice — who told you about that? *(Prentice is immobile.)* Prentice? *(Shakes him.)* Mr. Prentice? *(No move.)* Mr. Prentice? *(To Derek.)* He's not...

DEREK: *(Kneels.)* Prentice?

VINNY: Oh my God.

DEREK: Mr. Prentice. Come on, wake up.

VINNY: He doesn't seem to be...

DEREK: *(Stands back.)* Jesus. You must have hurt him when you...

VINNY: I hardly touched him. Is he alright? He said he had a weak heart...

DEREK: *(Moves away from him.)* Mr. Prentice, are you alright??

VINNY: Examine him!

DEREK: You examine him!

VINNY: Me? You're in the First Aid — you're the one with the stethoscope.

DEREK: Shut up about that! Mr. Prentice?

VINNY: Every Thursday you're practising for this kind of thing...

DEREK: I said shut up. Is he breathing at all?

VINNY: You mean you don't...?

DEREK: *(Quietly.)* Prentice, please open your eyes.

VINNY: But you must know something. You were at Hilary's birth, in the delivery room...

DEREK: *(Looking at Prentice.)* Jesus, he's not breathing.

VINNY: Remember the vegetable — how your son would have been a vegetable if you didn't tell the gynecologist...

DEREK: Will you shut up — I wasn't there.

VINNY: You were there...

DEREK: I wasn't! I was there at the beginning but then I fainted...

VINNY: Fainted?

DEREK: They had to carry me out...it was another doctor that Hilary heard shouting.

VINNY: What?!

DEREK: I have to say these things because she wants me to be a doctor...

VINNY: *(Angrily grabs Derek.)* What did you say?

DEREK: *(Angrily pulls free, as.)* Alright — for Christ sake, the guy she was going to marry was a doctor, so...

VINNY: So you know nothing?

DEREK: Prentice, please don't do this...

VINNY: And you wanted to be at Joan's delivery — keeping an eye on her things?

DEREK: I didn't! I don't want to be at anyone's delivery — I can't stand that sort of thing.

VINNY: Well, that's great — that's terrific — and now look at what you've done!

DEREK: *(Breaks down in sudden sobs of panic.)* Oh God, oh Christ, I'm ruined, destroyed...I'll be finished in the Club, on the Committee, the police will want to know...Hilary...her family...Oh God, oh Christ, I'm ruined...

VINNY: *(Suddenly taking over.)* Listen — stop! First of all, don't panic. *(Then.)* We'll say he fainted...

DEREK: Fainted? There's blood on his head.

VINNY: We'll say he hit his head...looking at the dogs...the way you did...and then he fainted.

DEREK: What? Yes. Right. We could say that...and that sounds right because I had said I wanted to check the security...so that's why we had the dogs on...

VINNY: Exactly. Then when Joan and Hilary get back, we can ask them to help us revive him...

DEREK: *(Panic.)* Revive him? How can they revive him if...?

VINNY: Stay calm!

DEREK: Right, right — I'm calm...

VINNY: Then when he doesn't come round for them, then we'll call a doctor...

DEREK: Right. Freddie Dawson. He's in the Club, on the Committee, chairman of the Residents' Association...

VINNY: Okay, but all the time we have to keep remembering that it was an accident...

DEREK: Oh right — no one meant for this to happen...

VINNY: He just happened to hit his head the way you did...

DEREK: Looking at the Security. Great. Fine. Well done. *(Then.)* And Vinny, when we get through this, I'll look after you in the Club, on the Committee, that sort of thing...

VINNY: Never mind that now...

DEREK: No, that's a promise — when we get the road through the estate, and we will...I'll see that you get all the Security contracts...

VINNY: Listen, let's get this done first...

DEREK: You're right...as I said before: it's not the mistakes we make, but how we correct them...and you really are Mr. Fix-It, Vinny — you really are one great Mr. Fix-It.

VINNY: Right. Now maybe you should be examining him.

DEREK: *(Panic.)* Not if he's...

VINNY: They'll come in thinking he's fainted.

DEREK: Oh right. Right. I hate doing this.

(Takes out his stethoscope. Then puts it to Prentice's chest.)

DEREK: Oh God, not a sound. He really is, you know — I know that much. *(Takes it away. Vinny will now busily take Mr. Prentice's glasses from the table and carefully place them on Mr. Prentice's face. Then he will tidy the door and close the window — all as:)*

VINNY: When did you get that thing anyway?

DEREK: Years ago — to convince Hilary about the Thursdays.

VINNY: Desperate carry-on.

DEREK: Don't start that.

VINNY: I'm not, I'm not. *(Then.)* And what about all the trophies you won.

DEREK: Bought them. Had them all engraved myself. *(Then.)* But we were always so bloody careful.

VINNY: Picking her up in the street?

DEREK: It was in the council houses. And we always cleared off — I always insisted we go to Gaston's Hotel.

VINNY: Gaston's Hotel? — that must be forty miles away....

DEREK: Exactly — and we always called ourselves Mr. and Mrs. Matthews. Well, that was Patti's little joke — she said Matthews sounded like "mattress" and we always had Commodore mattresses in Gaston's.

VINNY: *(Coldly.)* Great sense of humour.

DEREK: *(Bitterly.)* When she wasn't cracking stupid jokes, she was trying to talk me into leaving Hilary.

VINNY: Leaving Hilary?

DEREK: Yeah — some chance I'd have of surviving, without Hilary's money. Stupid little bitch.

VINNY: *(Listens at the door).* Quick — start examining him.

DEREK: Right. I really hate this. *(Puts the stethoscope to Prentice's chest again.)* I had to stop listening to Patti's heart because the gurgling sound of it used to make me sick.

VINNY: And stop talking about her!

DEREK: *(Listens.)* Jesus — silence.

THE SHADOW OF A GUNMAN
by Sean O'Casey

SEUMAS
THE LANDLORD, MR. MULLIGAN

Seumas, a notions "pedlar" (age twenty-five), rooms with Maguire, a poet. As the scene opens, Seumas's day is off to a bad start: he's overslept, his suspenders break, a fellow salesman says he can't go on rounds as promised and, finally, Seumus receives a visit from the elderly landlord.

(Seumas goes over and opens the door. A man of about sixty is revealed, dressed in a faded blue serge suit; a half tall hat is on his head. It is evident that he has no love for Seumas, who denies him the deference he believes is due from a tenant to a landlord. He carries some papers in his hand.)

THE LANDLORD: *(Ironically.)* Good-day, Mr. Shields; it's meself that hopes you're feelin' well — you're lookin' well, anyhow — though you can't always go be looks nowadays.

SEUMAS: It doesn't matter whether I'm lookin' well or feelin' well; I'm all right, thanks be to God.

THE LANDLORD: I'm very glad to hear it.

SEUMAS: It doesn't matter whether you're glad to hear it or not, Mr. Mulligan.

THE LANDLORD: You're not inclined to be very civil, Mr. Shields.

SEUMAS: Look here, Mr. Mulligan, if you come here to raise an argument, I've something to do — let me tell you that.

THE LANDLORD: I don't come here to raise no argument; a person ud have small gains argufyin' with you — let me tell you that.

SEUMAS: I've no time to be standin' here gostherin' with you — let me shut the door, Mr. Mulligan.

THE LANDLORD: You'll not shut no door till you've heard what I've got to say.

SEUMAS: Well, say it then, an' go about your business.

THE LANDLORD: You're very high an' mighty, but take care you're not goin' to get a drop. What a baby you are not to know what brings me here! Maybe you thought I was goin' to ask you to come to tea.

SEUMUS: Are you goin' to let me shut the door, Mr. Mulligan?

THE LANDLORD: I'm here for me rent; you don't like the idea of bein' asked to pay your just an' lawful debts.

SEUMAS: You'll get your rent when you learn to keep your rent-book in a proper way.

THE LANDLORD: I'm not goin' to take any lessons from you, any-how.

SEUMAS: I want to have no more talk with you, Mr. Mulligan.

THE LANDLORD: Talk or no talk, you owe me eleven weeks' rent, an' it's marked down again' you in black an' white.

SEUMAS: I don't care a damn if it was marked down in green, white, an' yellow.

THE LANDLORD: You're a terribly independent fellow, an' it ud be fitter for you to be less funny an' stop tryin' to be billickin' honest an' respectable people.

SEUMAS: Just you be careful what you're sayin', Mr. Mulligan. There's law in the land still.

THE LANDLORD: Be me sowl there is, an' you're goin' to get a little of it now. *(He offers the papers to Seumas.)* Them's for you.

SEUMAS: *(Hesitating to talk them.)* I want to have nothing to do with you, Mr. Mulligan.

THE LANDLORD: *(Throwing the papers in the center of the room.)* What am I better? It was the sorry day I ever let you come into this house. Maybe them notices to quit will stop you writin' let-ters to the papers about me an' me house.

SEUMAS: *(Taking no notice.)* Writing letters to the papers is my busi-ness, an' I'll write as often as I like, when I like, an' how I like.

THE LANDLORD: You'll not write about this house at all events. You can blow about the state of the yard, but you took care to say nothin' about payin' rent: oh no, that's not in your line. But since you're not satisfied with the house, you can pack up an' go to another.

SEUMAS: I'll go, Mr. Mulligan, when I think fit, an' no sooner.

THE LANDLORD: Not content with keeping the rent, you're startin' to bring in lodgers...Bringin' in lodgers without as much as be your leave — what's the world comin' to at all that a man's house isn't his own? But I'll soon put a stop to your gallop, for on the twen-ty-eight of next month out you go, and there'll be few sorry to see your back.

SEUMAS: I'll go when I like.

THE LANDLORD: I'll let you see whether you own the house or no.

SEUMAS: I'll go when I like!

THE LANDLORD: We'll see about that.

SEUMAS: We'll see.

THE LANDLORD: Ay, we'll see.

(*The Landlord goes out and Seumas shuts the door.*)

THE LANDLORD: *(Outside.)* Mind you, I'm in earnest; you'll not stop in this house a minute longer than the twenty-eight.

SEUMAS: *(With a roar.)* Ah, go to hell!

JOHN BULL'S OTHER ISLAND
by George Bernard Shaw

DOYLE
BROADBENT

> *Tom Broadbent, an Englishman, and Larry Doyle, an Irishman, are*
> *partners in the business of civil engineering in Westminster, England.*
> *They are also "bachelors and bosom friends." This scene takes place*
> *just before 5:00 p.m. in the summer of 1904, shortly after Broadbent*
> *has hired a drunken Irishman to be his secretary on a trip to Ireland.*

DOYLE: *(Returning.)* Where the devil did you pick up that seedy
swindler? What was he doing here? *(He goes up to the table where
the plans are, and makes a note on one of them, referring to his
pocket book as he does so.)*

BROADBENT: There you go! Why are you so down on every
Irishman you meet, especially if he's a bit shabby? poor devil!
Surely a fellow-countryman may pass you the top of the morning
without offence, even if his coat is a bit shiny at the seams.

DOYLE: *(Contemptuously.)* The top of the morning! Did he call you
the broth of a boy? *(He comes to the writing table.)*

BROADBENT: *(Triumphantly.)* Yes.

DOYLE: And wished you more power to your elbow?

BROADBENT: He did.

DOYLE: And that your shadow might never be less?

BROADBENT: Certainly.

DOYLE: *(Taking up the depleted whisky bottle and shaking his head at
it.)* And he got about half a pint of whisky out of you.

BROADBENT: It did him no harm. He never turned a hair.

DOYLE: How much money did he borrow?

BROADBENT: It was not borrowing exactly. He shewed a very hon-
orable spirit about money. I believe he would share his last
shilling with a friend.

DOYLE: No doubt he would share his friend's last shilling if his friend
was fool enough to let him. How much did he touch you for?

BROADBENT: Oh, nothing. An advance on his salary — for travelling
expenses.

DOYLE: Salary! In Heaven's name, what for?

BROADBENT: For being my Home Secretary, as he very wittily called it.

DOYLE: I dont see the joke.

BROADBENT: You can spoil any joke by being cold-blooded about it. I saw it all right when he said it. It was something — something really very amusing — about the Home Secretary and the Irish Secretary. At all events, he's evidently the very man to take with me to Ireland to break the ice for me. He can gain the confidence of the people there, and make them friendly to me. Eh? *(He seats himself on the office stool, and tilts it back so that the edge of the standing desk supports his back and prevents his toppling over.)*

DOYLE: A nice introduction, by George! Do you suppose the whole population of Ireland consists of drunken begging letter writers, or that even if it did, they would accept one another as references?

BROADBENT: Pooh! nonsense! he's only an Irishman. Besides, you dont seriously suppose that Haffigan can humbug me, do you?

DOYLE: No: he's too lazy to take the trouble. All he has to do is sit there and drink your whisky while you humbug yourself. However, you neednt argue about Haffigan, for two reasons. First, with your mother in his pocket he will never reach Paddington: There are too many public houses on the way. Second, he's not an Irishman at all.

BROADBENT: Not an Irishman! *(He is so amazed by the statement that he straightens himself and brings the stool bolt upright.)*

DOYLE: Born in Glasgow. Never was in Ireland in his life. I know all about him.

BROADBENT: But he spoke — he behaved just like an Irishman.

DOYLE: Like an Irishman!! Man alive, dont you know that all this top-of-the-morning and broth-of-a-boy and more-power-to-your-elbow business is got up in England to fool you, like the Albert Hall concerts of Irish music? No Irishman ever talks like that in Ireland, or ever did, or ever will. But when a thoroughly worthless Irishman comes to England, and finds the whole place full of romantic duffers like you, who will let him loaf and drink and sponge and brag as long as he flattens your sense of moral superiority by playing the fool and degrading himself and his country, he soon learns the antics that take you in. He picks them up at the theatre or the music hall. Haffigan learnt the rudiments from his father, who came from my part of Ireland. I knew his uncles, Matt and Andy Haffigan of Rosscullen.

BROADBENT: *(Still incredulous.)* But his brogue?

DOYLE: His brogue! A fat lot you know about brogues! Ive heard you call a Dublin accent that you could hang a hat on, a brogue. Heaven help you! you don't know the difference between Connemara and Rathmines. *(With violent irritation.)* Oh, damn Tim Haffigan! lets drop the subject: he's not worth wrangling about.

BROADBENT: Whats wrong with you today, Larry? Why are you so bitter? *(Doyle looks at him perplexedly; comes slowly to the writing table; and sits down at the end next to the fireplace before replying.)*

DOYLE: Well: your letter completely upset me, for one thing.

BROADBENT: Why?

DOYLE: Your foreclosing this Rosscullen mortgage and turning poor Nick Lestrange out house and home has rather taken me aback; for I liked the old rascal when I was a boy and had the run of his park to play in. I was brought up on the property.

BROADBENT: But he wouldnt pay the interest. I had to foreclose on behalf of the Syndicate. So now I'm off to Rosscullen to look after the property myself. *(He sits down at the writing table opposite Larry, and adds, casually, but with an anxious glance at his partner.)* Youre coming with me, of course?

DOYLE: *(Rising nervously and recommencing his restless movements.)* Thats it. Thats what I dread. Thats what has upset me.

BROADBENT: But dont you want to see your country again after 18 years absence? to see your people? to be in the old home again? to —

DOYLE: *(Interrupting him very impatiently.)* Yes, yes: I know all that as well as you do.

BROADBENT: Oh well, of course *(With a shrug.)* if you take it in that way, I'm sorry.

DOYLE: Never you mind my temper: it's not meant for you, as you ought to know by this time. *(He sits down again, a little ashamed of his petulance; reflects a moment bitterly; then bursts out.)* I have an instinct against going back to Ireland: an instinct so strong that I'd rather go with you to the South Pole than to Rosscullen.

BROADBENT: What! Here you are, belonging to a nation with the strongest patriotism! the most inveterate homing instinct in the world! and you pretend youd rather go anywhere than back to Ireland. You dont suppose I believe you, do you? In your heart—

DOYLE: Never mind my heart: an Irishman's heart is nothing but his imagination. How many of all those millions that have left Ireland have ever come back or wanted to come back? But whats the use of talking to you? Three verses of twaddle about the Irish emigrant "sitting on the stile, Mary", or three hours of Irish patriotism in Bermondsey or the Scotland Division of Liverpool, go further with you than all the facts that stare you in the face. Why, man alive, look at me! You know the way I nag, and worry, and carp, and cavil, and disparage, and am never satisfied and never quiet, and try the patience of my best friends.

BROADBENT: Oh, come Larry! do yourself justice. Youre very amusing and agreeable to strangers.

DOYLE: Yes, to strangers. Perhaps if I was a bit stiffer to strangers and a bit easier at home, like an Englishman, I'd be better company for you.

BROADBENT: We get on well enough. Of course you have the melancholy of the Celtic race —

DOYLE: *(Bounding out of his chair.)* Good God!!!

BROADBENT: *(Slyly.)* — and also its habit of using strong language when theres nothing the matter.

DOYLE: Nothing the matter! When people talk about the Celtic race, I feel as if I could burn down London. That sort of rot does more harm than ten Coercion Acts. Do you suppose a man need be a Celt to feel melancholy in Rosscullen? Why, man, Ireland was peopled just as England was; and its breed was crossed by just the same invaders.

BROADBENT: True. All the capable people in Ireland are of English extraction. It has often struck me as a most remarkable circumstance that the only party in parliament which shews the genuine old English character and spirit is the Irish party. Look at its independence, its determination, its defiance of bad Governments, its sympathy with oppressed nationalities all the world over! How English!

DOYLE: Not to mention the solemnity with which it talks old fashioned nonsense which it know perfectly well to be a century behind the times. Thats English, if you like.

BROADBENT: No, Larry, no. You are thinking of the modern hybrids that now monopolize England. Hypocrites, humbugs, Germans, Jews, Yankees, foreigners, Park Laners, cosmopolitan riffraff. Dont call them English. They dont belong to the dear old island, but to their confounded new empire; and by George! theyre worthy of it; and I wish them joy of it.

DOYLE: *(Unmoved by this outburst.)* There! You feel better now, dont you?

BROADBENT: *(Defiantly.)* I do. Much better.

PERMISSIONS ACKNOWLEDGEMENTS